The Chakrasamvara Root Tantra

The material in this book is strictly intended for those who have received the proper empowerments.

THE DECHEN LING PRACTICE SERIES

THE CHAKRASAMVARA ROOT TANTRA

The Speech of Glorious Heruka

Translated by David Gonsalez

Wisdom Publications
199 Elm Street
Somerville, MA 02144 USA
wisdomexperience.org

Library of Congress Cataloging-in-Publication Data
Names: Gonsalez, David, 1964–2014, translator.
Title: The Chakrasamvara root tantra: the speech of glorious Heruka / translated by David
    Gonsalez.
Other titles: Tripiṭaka. Sūtrapiṭaka. Tantra. Cakrasaṃvaratantra. English.
Description: First Wisdom edition. | Somerville, MA: Wisdom Publications, [2020] |
    Series: The Dechen Ling practice series | Previously published by Dechen Ling Press
    under the title Heruka Root Tantra.
Identifiers: LCCN 2020019203 (print) | LCCN 2020019204 (ebook) |
    ISBN 9781614295396 (hardcover) | ISBN 9781614295570 (ebook)
Classification: LCC BQ2180.C3522 E5 2020 (print) | LCC BQ2180.C3522 (ebook) |
    DDC 294.3/823—dc23
LC record available at https://lccn.loc.gov/2020019203
LC ebook record available at https://lccn.loc.gov/2020019204

ISBN 978-1-61429-539-6   ebook ISBN 978-1-61429-557-0

24 23 22 21 20
5 4 3 2 1

A previous edition of this book published by Dechen Ling Press had the title
as *Heruka Root Tantra* on the title page.
The illustration of Heruka in the color insert is © 2020 Andy Weber.
Cover artwork: *The Mahasiddhas, Tilopa and Naropa*, courtesy of Rubin Museum of Art.
Cover and interior design by Gopa & Ted2, Inc. Set in Perpetua MT Pro 12/14.5.
Printed on acid-free paper that meets the guidelines for permanence and durability of the
Production Guidelines for Book Longevity of the Council on Library Resources.

Printed in Canada.

Contents

Publisher's Note to the New Edition

It is a pleasure for Wisdom Publications to bring out the *Dechen Ling Practice Series*. Ven. Losang Tsering provided a great kindness to qualified practitioners when he made available in English these incredible texts, which combine the depth of Madhyamaka philosophy with the sophistication of Vajrayana practices, as found in Lama Tsongkhapa's rich tradition.

Some time ago, I expressed to Ven. Losang Tsering that these texts had been helpful in my own practice, and this led to conversations about Dechen Ling Press collaborating with Wisdom Publications. Not long before Ven. Losang Tsering passed, we both agreed that Wisdom Publications would be an excellent place to preserve the legacy of these books and make them available to practitioners throughout the world. I am very happy to see the fruition of our intentions. May this series be a support for practitioners under the guidance of qualified teachers.

Daniel Aitken

Translator's Introduction

A FAMOUS TIBETAN aphorism says, "The practice of tantra is accomplished through faith and imagination." It is with these two mental factors that we must approach this text. I am not attempting to present a critical examination of the origins of the *Chakrasamvara Tantra*, also known as the *Heruka Tantra*, or its social implications. Instead this work is intended for Buddhist practitioners who wish to study and practice the teachings of Heruka as preserved in the Tibetan Buddhist tradition. A cynical mind that believes in nothing other than empirical knowledge requires little imagination and virtually no faith. In the practice of tantra we are asked to believe in something that is not directly evident to our senses. At present our perception of ourselves and the world around us is largely determined by our sense faculties. We often don't question the role that we ourselves play in our experiences, much less our perception of and reaction to our experiences.

In the practice of tantra there are two primary obstacles we are constantly working to overcome—namely, ordinary conceptions and ordinary appearances. These two are the obstructions to liberation and the obstructions to omniscience, respectively. In the beginning these two are primarily accomplished through faith and imagination and later replaced with pure conceptions and pure appearances. Therefore, as practitioners of tantra we must try to transcend the limitations of our ordinary perceptions and believe, if only for a while, that a world of enlightened beings full of magic and mystery is indeed possible. It is only then that we will begin to experience for ourselves the great key that tantra holds to unlock the door to a higher perception of reality.

With this in mind I would like you to remain open to the possibility of the wonders of this tantra—to the complete transformation of our mundane existence into an active engagement with the reality of Chakrasamvara.

The Origins of Heruka[1]

There are two origins of the teachings of Heruka: the ancient and the modern. The ancient teaching was requested by Vajrapani and Vajravarahi and taught by Vajradhara at the peak of Mount Meru.[2] The modern was taught by Buddha Shakyamuni in his tantric aspect as Vajradhara, who emanated as Chakrasamvara, bestowed the empowerment, and taught the tantra at the request of Vajrapani in Palden Drepung (Skt. Shri Dhanyakataka Caitya) in southern India.

Prior to Buddha Shakyamuni's enlightenment, this world was under the control of Maha-Ishvara. Ishvara and his consort Kalarati had four primary aspects: peaceful, increasing, controlling, and wrathful. The wrathful aspect dwelt atop Mount Meru and held dominion over our world and over the twenty-four sacred sites in particular. The practitioners devoted to Ishvara engaged in negative actions for the purpose of pleasing Ishvara and thus created great negative karma. Due to his great compassion and at the request of Vajrapani and Vajravarahi, Buddha Vajradhara emanated in an aspect similar to Ishvara and subjugated him. Taking up Ishvara's hand-implements and attire, both Ishvara and Kalarati offered themselves as cushions for Heruka's feet. Heruka sent emanations into the twenty-four sacred sites and subjugated the Ishvara deities dwelling in those places.

1. Here, the origins of the *Chakrasamvara Tantra* are described following traditional teachings transmitted by Buddhist scholars and practitioners in Tibet.
2. According to ancient Indian cosmology, Mount Meru is the center of our universe and is formed of various precious jewels. It is irrelevant whether this cosmological model is accurate or not, as I am sure this description would be updated if the teachings of Heruka were being given in the twenty-first century. What is important to keep in mind is that the center of our universe, whatever that may be, is the abode of Heruka. It is also worth noting that while there are numerous similarities between various Buddhist and Hindu practices and deities, this fact is not being denied. Instead, just as any modern exposition of a religious system would no doubt be affected and interpreted in the light of the modern scientific model and religious standards, in the same way the teaching of Chakrasamvara was interpreted and expounded within the religious, scientific, and social standards of its time.

These sacred sites then became the holy places of Heruka. To this day practitioners of Ishvara and Kalarati as well as Heruka and Vajrayogini make pilgrimages to these holy places.

It is said that various other buddhas assisted Heruka in his subjugation of Ishvara and his retinue. For instance, Akshobhya emanated as Heruka's celestial mansion; Ratnasambhava emanated as the twenty-four deities in his retinue; Amitabha emanated as the four dakinis of the wheel of great bliss and the eight goddesses of the corners and directions; Amoghasiddhi emanated as the six armor deities of the father and mother, comprising twelve in all; and finally, Vairochana emanated as the seventeen deities for blessing the aggregates, elements, and sources, thus completing the sixty-two deities of Heruka's retinue.

According to Lama Tsongkhapa's *Clear Illumination of All Hidden Meaning*, there are three root tantras of Heruka. The longest version consists of three hundred thousand verses; the middle-length version has one hundred thousand verses; and the shortest root tantra—the version translated here—has seven hundred verses divided into fifty-one chapters. Only the latter version, it is said, was translated from Sanskrit into Tibetan.

These are called *root tantras* because they were the first discourses given by the Buddha on the practice of Chakrasamvara and it is from these three that all other teachings of Chakrasamvara have arisen. Thus they are like the "root" of the Chakrasamvara teachings in this world. There are also five explanatory tantras that help clarify various aspects of this *Chakrasamvara Root Tantra*.

Based on the *Root Tantra*, the explanatory tantras, and the genius of the Indian mahasiddhas, three primary lineages of Heruka emerged—namely, those of Luipa, Krishnapada, and Ghantapa. It is said that Luipa's tradition is the most extensive; Krishnapada's tradition emphasizes the tantric activities; and Ghantapa's tradition is unique because of its empowerment into the body mandala. While all three have body mandala practices, only Ghantapa's tradition has a separate empowerment into the body mandala. While Luipa's tradition is maintained in the Gelukpa tantric colleges, Gyumé and Gyutö, Ghantapa's lineage is the favorite among yogis and yoginis. Krishnapada's lineage is not as widespread as the first two. However, in general there have been literally hundreds of Tibetan commentaries on the practice of Heruka.

As it says in the extensive dedication prayer composed by Lama Tsongkhapa,

> The meaning of the root tantra of Chakrasamvara
> Was explained well in dependence upon the explanatory tantras,
> And the oral instructions of Supreme Siddha Ghantapa
> Who collected the essence of that excellent teaching.[3]

Divisions of Highest Yoga Tantra

Within highest yoga tantra there are two primary classifications: mother tantra and father tantra. The mother tantras emphasize the attainment of the most subtle mind of clear light—realizing emptiness. The father tantras emphasize the attainment of the illusory body, which is composed of the most subtle energy-wind inseparable from the mind of clear light that arises in the aspect of the deity. The clear light ultimately transforms into the dharmakaya and the illusory body transforms into the sambhogakaya, from which the nirmanakaya manifests.

The mother tantras, particularly the *Chakrasamvara Root Tantra*, are also referred to as the *yogini tantras*, with emphasis placed on the yoginis. These female beings are sometimes depicted as enlightened beings, at other times as manifestations of enlightened beings, and yet at other times as ordinary women of various dispositions and levels of spiritual maturity. There are several chapters in the *Root Tantra* that discuss the characteristics of the dakinis and of Vajravarahi in particular. Yet this is not the primary distinction between father and mother tantras. Instead we must look to the practices that primarily give rise to either the clear light or the illusory body as the characteristics that define the mother and father tantras, respectively.

Benefits of Heruka Practice

When the Buddha expounded other tantras, the mandalas were dissolved at the conclusion of the empowerment. However, Buddha Vajradhara did

3. Tsongkhapa, quoted in Pabongkha Dechen Nyingpo, *Increasing the Realization of Great Bliss*, trans. David Gonsalez (Seattle: Dechen Ling Press, 2002; 2007).

not withdraw the mandala of Heruka but instead left it intact as a countermeasure to the negative energy of Ishvara and his retinue. Thus, atop Mount Meru and in the twenty-four sacred sites there still remain the entire supporting and supported Chakrasamvara mandalas.

Therefore, practitioners of Heruka and Vajrayogini receive blessings much more swiftly; these blessings are also more powerful than those received from other deities. Since Vajradhara left the mandala as a countermeasure to the negative influence of Ishvara, and because Ishvara thrives on negative energy itself, this means that the more degenerate the times become, the more powerful the blessings of Heruka will be. Additionally, there are countless emanations of Heruka, Vajrayogini, and their retinue in the world; thus it is very easy to meet with an emanation of Heruka or Vajrayogini who will assist us in our spiritual practice.

The name *Chakrasamvara* means "binding all wheels" and indicates that all phenomena or "wheels" are "bound" within the dharmakaya—that is, the omniscient mind of Chakrasamvara. *Wheels* can also refer to the "wheels" within Heruka's mandala, such as the five wheels that constitute the Heruka mandala: the commitment wheel, the body, speech, and mind wheels, and the wheel of great bliss.

In chapter 41 of the *Chakrasamvara Root Tantra*, it says,

However many other places there are,
They are the yoginis of the mandala of
The glorious Heruka.

Shri Heruka, the great churner,
The principal mother of that mandala,
And these twenty-four dakinis,
Pervade all migrators in the three worlds,
All things animate and inanimate.

It is also taught in the *Root Tantra* that wherever there is a practitioner of Heruka, that place becomes hallowed ground inhabited by Heruka. By merely visiting or making offerings to such places, one creates merit equal to having made offerings to all the buddhas.

As it says in chapter 29 of the *Root Tantra*,

Whatever place is inhabited
By a yogi or supreme hero,
Even low caste or barbarian,
That region is a favored one.
In order to care for living beings
I shall always abide there.

Regarding the power of reciting the mantra of Heruka, in chapter 29 it says,

[If] you always recite the root mantra,
You will accomplish all of your desires.
All the demons will act very peacefully and
The moving and unmoving in the three worlds—
A treasure of the fruit of the play of yoga—
Arise from this secret mantra.

Regarding the close essence mantra of Heruka, chapter 12 of the *Root Tantra* states,

Next, the close essence [mantra]:
It is taught that all attainments
Will be obtained and
Everything in all three worlds
Will be accomplished in an instant.

There are limitless good qualities that can be attained through the practice of Heruka, such as pacifying, increasing, controlling, and wrathful actions. One can even attain magical abilities, such as making oneself invisible, the power of flight, and of course, the supreme attainment of enlightenment.

In chapter 27 it says,

It is not possible to explain
The pure merits that occur or
The extensive good qualities of the practitioner.

> How could one express
> With only one mouth
> What cannot be explained
> Even with a hundred thousand mouths?

It is also said that anyone who sees, hears, touches, or even thinks of a Heruka practitioner will accumulate great merit and purify negative karma. As stated in chapter 1,

> The yogi himself is the supreme [field of] merit,
> Since by seeing, touching,
> Hearing, or remembering [him],
> [One] becomes liberated from all nonvirtues.
> About this itself you should have no doubt.

Also, by merely reciting the *Root Tantra* one attains great merit and purifies great stores of negative karma. In chapter 51 it says,

> For example, if a container filled with butter
> Is placed in the middle of a fire,
> The fresh butter on top will melt and
> Destroy the impurities of that container.
> In the same way, Shri Heruka
> Will destroy the signs of nonvirtue.
>
> By merely remembering, concentrating,
> Reading, reciting, or writing,
> You will attain the enjoyments of the pure lands
> Or the state of a chakravartin king.

There are countless benefits that stem from the practice of Heruka. For example, if you receive the empowerment and maintain the commitments, at the time of your death you will be led to the pure land of the dakinis by Heruka, Vajrayogini, and a host of dakas and dakinis. As chapter 51 declares,

The yogi will be transferred [to the pure land] with
The *Blood Drinker* as well as the yogini,
With a variety of flowers held in their hands,
Possessing a variety of victory banners and pendants,

With the sound of a variety of music,
And offering various sounds, [they]
Will lead you to the pure land of the dakinis.
In this way death will be a [mere] conceptualization.

Though these benefits may appear to be overestimations of the power of
the *Root Tantra*, nevertheless we should not lose faith. Instead, we should
maintain our practice with unwavering devotion. For, as it also says in
chapter 51,

On this earth it is difficult to find
This great tantra of the most glorious Heruka.
For those who know of this yet lack faith,
Those poor beings will be tormented.
For them suffering will always arise.

Of course, as in all tantric practice, it is imperative that one receive the
complete empowerment of Chakrasamvara before engaging in the practice itself. As it says in chapter 3,

If the mantrika has not seen the mandala
Yet wishes to be a yogi,
This is like trying to strike the sky with his fist
Or drinking the water of a mirage.

After receiving the empowerment, it is essential that one maintain
the commitments taken at the time of the empowerment. As it says in
chapter 1,

The practitioner with perfect mental stabilization
Should always protect the spiritual commitments.
By damaging the commitments,

[That one] will not attain the realizations
From empowerment in the mandala.

With this as a basis one must then follow the guidance of a qualified lama. Attempting to undertake these practices without the guidance of a lama is a recipe for disaster. Krishnapada, the tantric master and an important lineage guru in the practice of Chakrasamvara, had to ask his lama for years before being given permission to engage in some of the more esoteric practices explained in this text.[4] Therefore, I wholeheartedly implore anyone interested in these practices to approach their own lama and request instruction. Also, it is possible that the meanings of the verses of the *Root Tantra* may vary. Sometimes the language is explicit, and other times the meaning is deeply embedded and expressed in symbolic language. Often there is more than one possible reading and a lama may only give you the meaning he feels you are spiritually prepared for, but later reveal to you a more profound reading that indicates more advanced levels of practice. Therefore, it is imperative that you learn the meaning appropriate to your level of spiritual training from your lama.

What follows is a very provisional outline of the text.

Summary of the *Chakrasamvara Root Tantra*

1. *The Deities*
2. *Various Mantras*
3. *Ritual Practices*
4. *Characteristics of the Dakinis*
5. *Secret Hand Gestures and Language*
6. *Generation Stage Practices*
7. *Vows and Commitments*
8. *Vajrayogini Practices*

1. *The Deities*
Of course, the primary deity of the *Root Tantra* is Heruka Chakrasamvara. Although he is described in various aspects, his primary aspect is

---

4. *Taranatha's Life of Krsnacarya/Kanha*, trans. David Templeman (Dharamsala: Library of Tibetan Works and Archives, 1989).

four faced and twelve armed. The other principal deities are the dakas and dakinis of the twenty-four sacred sites. These are primarily explained in chapters 4, 41, and 48, where their mantras are also revealed. Also of primary importance are the armor deities. There are other various deities of lesser significance that appear throughout the tantra.

2. *Various Mantras*

The mantras in the *Root Tantra* are revealed in a variety of ways. In chapters 5, 6, and 7 there is a very elaborate system for concealing the mantras through using a diagram that is drawn on the ground with each of the Sanskrit vowels and consonants placed in squares. The *Root Tantra* then explains the system for extracting each syllable from each square to construct the mantras. Although this system of concealment, which is also employed in chapter 30 in conjunction with the "mantra of the four faces," was used primarily as a way to prevent noninitiates from learning the mantras, it is also a ritual in itself.

There are also less conspicuous methods, such as those described in chapters 8, 12, and 48, where the mantras are simply arranged in reverse order. In chapter 50 the mantra is arranged in its proper order, as in chapter 25, where the root mantra is revealed with the "Eight-Line Praise to Heruka" added to the beginning. In some traditions the root mantra is recited with the "Eight-Line Praise" and in others the root mantra is recited without it.

There are four primary mantras of Heruka practice, called the *four precious mantras*. These are the root mantra, the essence mantra and close essence mantra of Heruka father and mother, and the armor mantras.

In chapter 8 it says,

> If on this earth there are the four precious [mantras],
> This is the sacred mantra rosary.
> The great knowledge of the dakinis is
> Heruka, the *King of Knowledge*.

3. *Ritual Practices*

The ritual practices occupy a relatively large portion of the *Root Tantra*. These chapters explain how to attain everything from the power of flight to subjugating a king and overthrowing his kingdom. It should also be noted that in many instances the use of wrathful or controlling actions that may be interpreted as nonvirtuous in nature are transformed into a means of enlightenment by the highly accomplished tantric adept. However, attempting to practice any of these without the proper spiritual maturity and guidance from one's lama is a sure cause for rebirth in the lower realms of existence, where even the word *happiness* will not be heard for an inconceivable period of time. In particular, in chapters 2 and 3 there is an explanation of entering the mandala and receiving empowerment as well as the respect and offering that should be paid to the tantric master. Also, throughout the chapters on ritual practice there are various explanations for relying upon an *action mudra*, or physical consort, which should only be undertaken by the highly realized and under the guidance of one's lama.

This being said, it is obvious that all of the magical powers and various attainments discussed in the *Root Tantra* are only attained after having attained very high levels of spiritual realization. It is only after having completed the retreat and subsequent fire offering, carried out with impeccable, single-pointed concentration and such strong divine pride and clear appearance, that you truly believe with every fiber of your being that you *are* the deity and begin to accomplish some of the attainments mentioned in the *Root Tantra*.

In his commentary on the *Kalachakra Tantra*, Geshe Ngawang Dhargyey says,

> This threatening mudra is a very powerful one when it is used by a highly accomplished person on the stage of completion. For example, such a practitioner could sit here, point this mudra at a far-off fruit tree, and he would be able to draw the fruit of that tree to himself. Then he could reverse the whole process and send the fruits back to their respective branches.[5]

5. Geshe Ngawang Dhargyey, *Commentary on the Kālacakra Tantra,* trans. Allan Wallace (Dharamsala: Library of Tibetan Works and Archives, 1985).

4. *Characteristics of the Dakinis*

There are several chapters that discuss the characteristics of the dakinis, from their physical characteristics to their mental dispositions. In this way one is able to identify whether a woman has the characteristics to potentially be an emanation of a dakini. This can also refer to her karmic disposition, which indicates the dakini and lineage with which she has the greatest karmic connection and also determines whether or not she is appropriate for one's own spiritual lineage, as revealed at the time of one's initiation.

5. *Secret Hand Gestures and Language*

These chapters reveal the hand and bodily gestures as well as the so-called dakini language with which one can communicate with dakinis. There are two possibilities here: first, that the woman is an actual emanation of a dakini; or second, that she has been initiated into the practice of Chakrasamvara and learned this secret form of communication. Either way this allows one to identify a woman with which one shares a sacred bond of tantric practice.

6. *Generation and Completion-Stage Practices*

Generation and completion-stage practices are scattered throughout the tantra. They are in many chapters, especially chapters 32 and 51. The completion stage is concealed throughout the *Root Tantra* through a variety of uses of ambiguous language. It is on the basis of the *Root Tantra* that the great mahasiddhas created their completion-stage systems, such as those described in the *Five Stages of the Completion Stage* of the mahasiddha Ghantapa and in the *Four Great Yogas* of Luipa.

7. *Vows and Commitments*

While this section could be subsumed under the "Generation and Completion-Stage Practices" or the "Characteristics of Dakinis," since vows and commitments are so important I have given them a separate heading for the sake of this introduction. They are found in various places throughout the *Root Tantra*, primarily chapters 26, 28, and 38. In chapter 26 appear the "eight uncommon commitments of mother tantra," which all Heruka and Vajrayogini practitioners will have memorized. Of particular importance is the *left-side conduct*, which refers to beginning all activities, particularly ritual actions, from the left. There are numerous other commitments mentioned in various places throughout the tantra. In chapter 38, the dire consequences of not keeping one's spiritual commitments are explained in bone-chilling detail.

8. *Vajrayogini Practices*
The Vajrayogini practices are in chapters 47 and 48. Here, the mantra of Vajrayogini is revealed as well as the extraordinary qualities and benefits of her mantra and practice.

This outline of eight sections is in no way a definitive summation of the *Root Tantra*; it is merely a way of introducing the material to facilitate a better understanding of the text as a whole.

Translation Considerations

The language in the *Chakrasamvara Root Tantra* is intentionally obscure and a means of protecting the tantra from being practiced by noninitiates. This system, while frustrating at times, serves its purpose and forces us to look to our lama for clarification and instruction. There is a three-fold process that is demanded of any tantric practitioner. First, one must receive the complete empowerment of the particular tantra one wishes to practice; second, one must receive the oral transmissions of the texts to be studied and sadhanas to be recited; and third, one needs the oral instructions and pith instructions that reveal the multifaceted meaning of that particular tantra. Only when fully equipped with these three—empowerment, transmission, and instructions—is one prepared to begin one's journey into the vast and profound ocean of tantric practice. With this in mind, I have desisted from heavily annotating the text and instead have left it in its own beautiful, poetic, and ambiguous language. In this way the reader will get a feeling of how the text reads in Tibetan and experience the flavor of the syntax.

Origins of This Translation

I first began working on this text in May 2001 with a photocopy of the *Root Tantra* that my guru, Gen Lobsang Choephel, obtained for me. As preparation for undertaking this translation, he gave me the transmission of Lama

Tsongkhapa's masterpiece *Clear Illumination of All Hidden Meaning,*[6] a commentary on the *Chakrasamvara Root Tantra.* Over the course of that year, I finished a rough draft of the translation. I then began working with my former Tibetan language teacher, Lobsang Thonden, who meticulously went over every word of the tantra with me. We then completed a more accurate translation. Nevertheless, I still had some questions, particularly about some of the terms and names used in the tantra. Over the next few years I had the good fortune to receive privately from Gen Lobsang Choephel the transmission of the following texts:

- Changkya Rolpay Dorjé's commentary on the generation stage of the body mandala in the tradition of Mahasiddha Ghantapa, entitled *Lamp Illuminating the Exalted Wisdom of Great Bliss.*
- Dakpo Rinpoche's commentary on the generation stage of Mahasiddha Ghantapa, entitled *Secret Path of the Method Vehicle: A Commentary on the Generation Stage of the Great Treasure of Blessing—Glorious Chakrasamvara in the Tradition of Mahasiddha Ghantapa.*
- Dakpo Rinpoche's commentary on the completion stage of the body mandala in the tradition of Mahasiddha Ghantapa, entitled *Detailed Commentary on the Five Stages of the Completion Stage of Chakrasamvara in the Tradition of Mahasiddha Ghantapa.*
- Panchen Losang Chökyi Gyaltsen's commentary to the completion stage of the body mandala in the tradition of Mahasiddha Ghantapa, entitled *Extremely Profound Commentary to the Five Stages of the Profound Tradition of the Powerful Siddha Ghantapa.*
- Pabongkha Rinpoche's commentary on the generation stage of the body mandala in the tradition of Mahasiddha Ghantapa, entitled *Gateway to the Ocean of Great Bliss.*
- Trijang Rinpoche's commentary on the generation stage and completion stage of the body mandala in the tradition of Mahasiddha Ghantapa, a text transcribed, edited, and compiled by Gen Lobsang Choephel from cassette tapes made during Trijang Rinpoche's teaching at the Library of Tibetan Works and Archives in 1973.
- Finally, from Gen Lobsang Choephel, I also received the transmission of the *Chakrasamvara Root Tantra* itself.

6. Tib. *Sbas don kun gsal.*

During this time I studied these and numerous other commentaries and continued looking for assistance from a translator who had command of both Tibetan and English, as well as knowledge of the *Root Tantra*, so that I could discuss my translation choices and the accuracy of the terminology. In June 2007, I received a scan of the *Root Tantra* from the Tibetan Buddhist Resource Center. This was an enormous help for two reasons. First of all, the scan of the text was perfectly clear, whereas the other text I had was a photocopy and many of the words were difficult to read; and second, this was a slightly different edition of the text.[7]

Finally, David Gray completed his annotated and critical translation of the *Chakrasamvara Tantra*. This was the final key I needed to complete my translation. There were still a few words about which I had questions, and these were addressed in Gray's text, and although they were different in style, our translations are very similar in meaning, which assured me that the translation was accurate.[8]

Tibetan Texts

For the first draft of this text, I relied upon a photocopy of an edition of Marpa Chökyi Wangchuk's translation of the *Root Tantra* as preserved in the Phugdrag edition of the Kangyur and published by the Library of Tibetan Works and Archives. This text was obtained for me by my guru, Gen Lobsang Choephel, expressly for the purpose of translating it. I also obtained a scan of the same text as preserved in the sTog Palace edition of the Kangyur from the Tibetan Buddhist Resource Center that contained slight variations.

Technical Note

I have not attempted to create a scholarly analysis of the *Root Tantra* but instead have simply tried to present a readable translation of the tantra for Buddhist practitioners.

---

7. For the origins of these two versions, see *Cakrasamvara Tantra (the Discourse of Śrī Heruka)*, trans. David Gray (New York: American Institute of Buddhist Studies at Columbia University, 2007).
8. All of the information that I gleaned from Gray's text is noted.

Where the Tibetan text is in verse, I tried to maintain the same structure, keeping the translation in verse as well. When dividing the verses into groups, I tried to follow the breaks as closely as possible, but as in many instances the Tibetan text may even exceed forty lines, I tried to break them up wherever possible to clarify the text. The prose section of the translation is in accordance with the structure of the Tibetan text.

While the term *Heruka*, in general, is often used to refer to wrathful deities, in this text it is used interchangeably with *Chakrasamvara*. The word *Lama* in Sanskrit is the name of one of four heart dakinis of the wheel of great bliss and should not be mistaken for the Tibetan word *lama* that is a translation of the Sanskrit word *guru*. I have italicized proper names and epithets such as *The Glorious Drinker of Blood* and so forth.

I have translated the Tibetan word *ngakpa* back to the Sanskrit *mantrika*, which simply means "a person who is a practitioner of tantra." Incidentally, the Tibetan word for such a person, *sgrub pa po*, could also be translated back into Sanskrit as *siddha*. But since *sgrub pa po* often refers to a person who is in the process of attaining realizations and not necessarily a person who has already attained such powers, I have opted to use *practitioner* instead of *siddha*. Those words or phrases that I myself have added for the sake of clarity have been set off in square brackets.

Object of accomplishment is a technical term used in tantric rituals to refer to the object of one's focus in the ritual and can refer to a variety of things. In the *Root Tantra*, however, it usually refers to a person who is being subjugated. Sometimes "hero" refers to Heruka and at other times refers to the practitioner of Heruka, the distinction being obvious from the context. There are other numerous terms that may not be immediately apparent. These should be clarified by receiving teachings directly from your own lama.

I have written the mantras the way my lamas have pronounced them, whose pronunciation is not necessarily always in accord with the Sanskrit. As this text is intended for Buddhist practitioners, it is my opinion that writing the mantras differently from the way they are pronounced by each practitioner's own lama can only lead to confusion. Anyone interested in learning the correct Sanskrit spelling can easily obtain such information. Also, when giving the names of the dakinis and so forth, I arranged them in phonetic Tibetan and set the Sanskrit in parentheses after each name.

While this will not appeal to scholars, nevertheless, it will make these names easy to pronounce. It is my hope that some practitioners will recite the *Root Tantra* as a devotional exercise and so the method I use should facilitate pronunciation. Any readers skilled in Tibetan language will easily be able to discern the correct Tibetan spelling.

In chapter 30 the *Root Tantra* reads, "Take the thirty-second *chart* ..." Here it really means to take the letter from the thirty-second *square*, referring to the forty-nine letters of the Sanskrit alphabet. Nevertheless, the Tibetan does say "chart" (*re mig*); therefore, I have not changed it to "square." From this short explanation you should be able to correctly identify the system for composing the mantras that are concealed in this fashion.

There are two editions of the *Chakrasamvara Root Tantra* that I employed for this translation. The colophons of both editions name the translator pair Prajnakirti and Marpa Chökyi Wangchuk (Tib. Mar pa Chos kyi dbang phyug), whose revised translation was based in turn on an earlier translation by Padmakara and Rinchen Zangpo.[9] One was published by the Library of Tibetan Works and Archives, based on the Phugdrag manuscript edition of the Kangyur; the other is the edition included in the sTog Palace edition of the Kangyur, which stems from a different recension of the Tibetan Buddhist canon.

Acknowledgments

I would like to thank Dr. David Gray, who encouraged me to continue with my translation when, in 2003, I discovered he was also working on a translation of the *Chakrasamvara Tantra*. I also contacted Dr. Gray in the final weeks of my work on the translation, and he was always gracious as well as brilliant.

I would like to thank Lobsang Thonden, who went over the entire text with me, checking my translation against the Tibetan.

I would also like to thank Keith Milton, who went over the entire text checking for spelling and grammatical errors as well as making suggestions to improve the text overall, as well as Julia Milton, who checked the introduction for similar corrections. And thanks to Glenn Mullin

---

9. Thanks to David Gray for assisting me in ascertaining the origins of these two editions.

for encouraging me to publish this text and helping me discern a proper translation for the phrasing that accompanies the title as stated at the end of each chapter. Glenn suggested "revelation of Shri Heruka," or simply "spoken by . . ." Since I had already chosen "spoken by," I used that. I would like to thank Vincent Montenegro for formatting this text.

Most of all I would like to thank all of my lamas who have guided me throughout the years, in particular Gen Lobsang Choephel, who bestowed numerous transmissions and commentaries throughout our long relationship and who is an extraordinary practitioner and scholar.

I would also like to thank Susan and David Heckerman for their continued support throughout the years, which affords me the opportunity to spend all my time translating or engaging in retreats as well as supporting various projects that I have undertaken throughout the years.

Herein Is Contained the Great Tantra of the Great Yogini, the Root Tantra of the Bhagawan Glorious Chakrasamvara in Fifty-One Chapters

(Shri-heruka-chakrasamvara-vidhana-yogi-niruttara-
sarvatantra-uttara-samvara-samgraha-nama)

The *King of Blood Drinkers* who is called *Chakrasamvara*,
the unexcelled tantra of all the yogini tantras, guru Heruka,
will be briefly explained.

1. Entering the Mandala

I prostrate to the Blessed One, glorious Vajrasattva.

Now I will explain the great secret,
Briefly but not extensively.

By the excellent union of Shri Heruka,
All of the desired aims will be obtained.
He surpasses the unsurpassed:
The net binding the dakinis.

If [you] delight in this supreme secret,
I will abide in the nature of all things.

The actual hero of all the dakinis,
Vajrasattva—Supreme Bliss—
[He] is the self-arisen Bhagavan Hero,
The net binding the dakinis.

It has arisen from the source of sound.
The sphere of activity is the practice of the commitments.
Abiding perfectly in the beginning, middle, and end,
In the three worlds [this tantra] is difficult to find.

The perfect union of the churner and the churned—
The mode of existence is like that.

Endowed with recitation of mantra and concentration,
Union itself is the ritual of exalted wisdom.
By listening to the explanation of
The yoga of this unexcelled tantra,

At special times the yogi should always
Make offerings to those endowed with the lineage,
The central, supreme, and pure breath,[10]
Together with scented water and so forth.

Accomplish the simultaneously born messengers,
Supreme, middling, or inferior;
By directing the mind inward
One should accomplish desire.

Make offerings with one's own substance, the drops,
To the buddhas and bodhisattvas.

The yogi himself is the supreme [field of] merit,
Since by seeing, touching,
Hearing, or remembering [him],
[One] becomes liberated from all nonvirtues.
About this itself you should have no doubt.

Pure actions destroy nonvirtues;
By secret mantra recitation and concentration, as well as
Through bliss, one achieves the attainments.

The practitioner with perfect mental stabilization
Should always protect the spiritual commitments.
By damaging the commitments,
[One] will not attain the realizations
From empowerment in the mandala.

10. This line is referring to extracting the wind from the central channel of the goddess.

By mixing honey, vermillion,[11]
Camphor, and red sandalwood
And placing [them] within the collection,
Hold the sign that represents all vajras.

By joining the tip of the thick with the back side,[12]
With knowledge of yoga, always enjoy [them].
By tasting it as if it were the peaceful drink[13]
Everlasting attainments will be obtained.

This [person] will not die for five [years];
It is the means of engaging all the attainments.

With the four offerings the great hero
[Fulfills] the wishes of the mind through
The two organs engaging in union;
Thus [you will] enter into union and sustain bliss.

The happiness of gods and humans gathered together
Could not compare to even a sixteenth
Of that produced in such a way
By the vajra holder.

The mountain, a jungle, a medicinal valley,
The banks of a great river, and
In a primordial charnel ground:
In these [places] draw the mandala.

FROM THE SPEECH OF GLORIOUS HERUKA, "ENTERING THE
MANDALA" IS THE FIRST CHAPTER.

---

11. The sTog Palace edition says "butter."
12. The "thick" is the thumb, and the "back side" is the ring finger.
13. According to Gray (2007, 160) this is *soma*, to which there are a variety of parallels in the context of the *Root Tantra*, most notably the inner offering and the secret substance distributed during the secret initiation.

2. The Ritual for Making Offerings to the Mandala

In that place anoint the ground of
The mandala with the unfallen cow dung
And the ashes of the charnel ground
Together with the five nectars.[14]

After anointing the ground,
In that place correctly construct the mandala,
And by means of visualizing that place, [imagine]
Everything is being performed in the charnel grounds.

A master endowed with all qualities should
Draw an excellent mandala
With powder from a charred, burned corpse
And bricks of a charnel ground.
One should have proper knowledge and understanding of tantra
And know the secret mantra of the *Glorious Drinker of Blood*.
Without anger, one should be clean, neat, learned, and
Know how to practice the perfection of wisdom.

With skulls adorning the crown of [your] head,
Smear [your] limbs with ash
And adorn your body with pure ornaments
And a bone rosary possessing the proper bones.

14. The Phugdrag edition says "with the man that died at half of ten."

With one piece adorning your crown
And with the bone rosary hanging down,
Holding the *khatvanga* staff in [your] hand,
You are the *Glorious Drinker of Blood*.

With mindfulness of the *Glorious Drinker of Blood*
Arrange a chakra at your heart.
Having armored oneself in such a way,
Arrange the fences in the directions.

Below that, arrange the weapons as well.
Place oneself within the mandala and
Above create a web of arrows.
Again, it is the nature of a dakini land.

Make a tent that becomes armor.
If [one] wears the armor in that way,
It cannot be destroyed even by the thirty-three [gods].

Thus, by being adorned with mantra and mudra
One has the supreme protection.
Draw the terrifying mandala
That bestows the supreme attainments.

Then, with a corpse-thread
or one moistened with great blood,
Draw the lines of the terrifying mandala,
The supreme palace of glorious Heruka,
One cubit, four cubits, or eight cubits.

All four doors have four corners,
And it is adorned with four gates.
The tantric practitioner should utilize a double [thread]
And make offerings to Heruka,
The net [binding] the dakinis.

In the center of that is a lotus
With petals, a blazing navel, and corolla.
The hero arranged in the center
Can terrify even Bhairava.
He is ablaze with extreme splendor
And the great laughter of HA HA,

Adorned with a rosary of human heads,
Three excellent eyes, and four powerful faces,
Gracefully wearing an elephant skin, and
Good eyebrows separated by a vajra,
His hands hold a katvanga and a human skull,
And he is gracefully adorned with a rosary of fifty [heads].

In front of glorious Heruka
Is the goddess Vajravarahi—
The most terrifying goddess—
With three wrathful eyes and a wrathful form.

Her skullcup is filled with intestines and
From her mouth blood drips out.
With a mudra she threatens in all directions
Gods, demigods, and humans.

Make offerings to the twenty-four dakinis
Who have arisen from the lineage of Vajravarahi
And abide in the center
And in the cardinal and intermediate directions.

Make offerings to the heroes as well
Who abide here perfectly in the mandala.
The practitioner who desires spiritual attainments
Should perform offerings to the nondual hero.

Next, accomplishing the vase:
Not being black, without a base, and so forth,

Fill it completely with such things as pearl, gold, jewels,
Coral, silver, copper, and all kinds of food.

Place a vessel upon it,
Tie a long thread around the neck, and
Adorn the mouth with a leaf.

Wrap each well with a pair of garments and
Arrange eight of them nicely at the doors, placing
The ninth in the center,
Well wrapped with a pair of garments.
Beautify each with gold or silver,
Pearl, or other jewels.

Beautify the mandala with gold
And every precious ornament.

If [you] worship in a delightful, supreme place,
Have no doubts [about] the attainments themselves.
With oneself in the door sprinkle perfectly scented water.
If you desire the supreme attainments,
Offer a hundred butter lamps.

The dakinis of the sky
Are arranged above by the mind.
Whichever dakinis are of the ground
Should all be arranged in the mandala.
Whichever dakinis go below the ground,
Arrange them below the ground.
Arrange all the female spirits in
The cardinal and intermediate directions.

If you desire the supreme attainments,
Offer incense, perfume, flowers and the like
According to the rituals.

Offer as well a hundred butter lamps
[To] Heruka abiding in the mandala,
Together with the heroes and yoginis.[15]

Offer red victory banners, yellow ones, and so forth,
As well as a variety of clothing in
White, black, and pale yellow,
And various flower garlands with
Canopies and pure vessel [cups].
In this way beautify [the mandala].

Thus with food and drink
And perfect concentration perform the offerings.

FROM THE SPEECH OF GLORIOUS HERUKA, "THE RITUAL
FOR MAKING OFFERINGS TO THE MANDALA" IS THE SECOND
CHAPTER.

15. This line is only in the sTog Palace edition.

3. The Good Qualities of the Ritual of Bestowing Empowerment

Next, the practitioner [should]
First please the spiritual master with all things.
Desiring attainments and with strong concentration
Make as many offerings to the guru as you are able.

Hanging the resounding bell,
Adorned with flowers and incense,
Cause the sweet sound of the bell to be heard.
The practitioner beats the drum
And proclaims HA HA.

Having made offerings to the mandala
With all desires, according to the ritual,
The face of that beautiful son should be
Covered with an excellent silken cloth
And his palms filled with flowers,
Then he should perfectly enter [the mandala].

With the practitioner in meditative stabilization
He should circumambulate [the mandala]
With a good mind of mental stabilization
And enter the magnificent palace.

With your body in the southern direction
Toss the flower with your hands
And cast it over the mandala.

Wherever the flower drops,
That reveals the place of Shri Heruka,
[Your] spiritual lineage and so forth.
Your name is then revealed by the master and
The name of that lineage becomes your name.

After that the excellent master abiding in
Meditative stabilization makes the offering of the mudra,
And on the next day the disciple
Should perfectly perform the actions.

By reciting three times over blood
[The master] forms it into a drop
And uncovers the face of the disciple
And should then reveal the mandala,
Showing perfectly the correct place
Of each deity of the palace.

Next the disciple perfectly bows
And once again circumambulates the master
Together with the palace,
Beginning from the left.
Afterward according to the ritual
Pay obeisance to the mandala and the guru.

Then make excellent offerings to the guru.
As in the teachings by the Tathagata, offer
One hundred thousand gold [coins]
And a variety of precious things,
A hundred pairs of clothing,
Horses, elephants, and the kingdom,
Earrings, bangles,
Necklaces, and excellent rings for the fingers,
A sacrificial thread made of gold,
Your excellent wife and daughter herself,
Male and female servants and [even] your sisters.

After making prostrations offer [these].
Thus according to the teachings the disciple
Should thoughtfully offer oneself to the guru
As well as all the other offerings.

From that time on you become a servant [of the Guru]
[Saying] "I offer myself to you as your servant."
Then things are perfectly arranged
By the practitioner according to the ritual,
Which pleases the dakinis and yoginis
[Such as] Dakini, Lama,
Khandaroha, and Rupini.

Whatever action you do and wherever you go
The practitioner should go together with dakinis.
If you accomplish this yoga
Have no doubt that whatever you do,
It will all be accomplished.

You will be unencumbered in the three worlds,
Become invisible, go underground and in the sky,
take the essence and be swift-footed.
Through merely wishing it, the practitioner
Can take rebirth as anything.

He can change his form into many things
And travel through space.
Even for the dakinis in particular, if the practitioner merely
Looks once at a migrating being
That being will certainly be subdued.

If the mantrika has not seen the mandala
Yet wishes to be a yogi,
This is like trying to strike the sky with his fist
Or drinking the water of a mirage.

This yoga is excellent and supreme.
It is the most sacred of all practices;
Whatever one desires will always arise.
You will be able to overpower[16]
Gods, demigods, and men.

It is said that [those who are bestowed]
Empowerment into this tantra
Will all become siddhas.

Through seeing, laughing, and holding hands,
Embracing each other and so forth
One should receive empowerment
On the crown of the head in
This most sacred of all tantras.
The glory of this [tantra] subdues gods and men.

This is the king of mandalas
That has not emerged nor will emerge in
The *Tattvasamgraha, Samvara,*
Guhyasamaja, or *Vajrabhairava.*[17]
Whatever is taught or not taught,
It all resides in the *Glorious Drinker of Blood.*

FROM THE SPEECH OF GLORIOUS HERUKA, "THE GOOD
QUALITIES OF THE RITUAL OF BESTOWING EMPOWERMENT"
IS THE THIRD CHAPTER.

16. Thanks to David Gray for help with this word.
17. For references to the texts in question, see Gray 2007, 176–77.

4. Establishing the Inseparability of the Heroes and Yoginis

Next the dakinis
Who abide magnificently:
Tsönchen (Mahavirya), Khorlo Gyurma (Chakravartini),
Tobchenma (Mahabala), Rab Pamo (Suvira),
Khorlö Gocha (Chakravarmini), Chang Tsongma (Shaundini), Dum
    Kyema (Khandaroha), Korlö Shuk (Cakravega).

Cha Dongma (Khaganana), Ta Namo (Hayakarna),
Shintu Sangmo (Subhadra), Jang Lhamo (Shyamadevi),
Chang Thungma (Surabhakshi), Lung Shukma (Vayuvega),
Likewise, Jikché Chenmo (Mahabhairava) and Sa Sungma (Airavati).

Shing Dribma (Drumacchaya), Langkai Wangchuk (Lankeshvari),
Mi-u Tungma (Kharvari), Pawö Loma (Viramati),
As well as Na Chenma (Mahanasa),
Ödenma (Prabhavati), Tum Mikma (Chandakshi),
And Rab Tumma (Prachanda).

These are the twenty-four dakinis
That have been previously established
In the centers of body, speech, and mind,
Internally just as they are externally.[18]

18. This line does not appear in the sTog Palace edition.

Recite the mantras which are their own names and
Attach HUM HUM PHAT at the end.

Seeing this excellent supreme yoga
Is like comparing fire to straw.
OM illuminates all [the mantras].
It bestows all the desired attainments.

Accomplish the hero himself
And view him within the mandala in a house,
And then by continuously meditating
[You] will accomplish the teachings of the Tathagata.

FROM THE SPEECH OF GLORIOUS HERUKA, "ESTABLISHING
THE INSEPARABILITY OF THE HEROES AND YOGINIS" IS THE
FOURTH CHAPTER.

5. The Ritual of Collecting the Letters of the Root Mantra

And then the source of all phenomena:
In the center of a variegated [lotus]
Is the indestructible and virtuous one.
The mantrika condenses all phenomena into one
And writes according to the ritual.

Here, these are the words of the mantra.
Prepare the Sanskrit vowels and consonants;
They are combined according to [their] class.

By knowing the division of the four of four and
The chart of the *Supreme Able One*
Abiding there, the hero is collected;
Bestowing the supreme attainment,
All the desired aims are achieved.

That which is the fifth of the fourth,
As well as the fifth of the fifth.
The fourth of the fifth, and
That which is the third of the first.
Likewise the twenty-ninth
And that which is the first of the fourth,
The fourth of the semivowels,[19] and
The second of that as well.

19. The term "semivowel" was taken from David Gray's translation.

The thirtieth is correctly extracted,
Likewise the twenty-sixth.
All of these are perfectly assembled.
Likewise half of half one hundred.
And then take the thirty-third,
The first of the first and
The third semivowel, and
The third of the first itself.
The thirty-second itself and
The fifth of the fourth,
The fourth of the fifth as well,
And the first semivowel.
The third of the second and
That which is the first of the third,
The fifth of the fifth,
The first of the first as well.
Likewise the eleventh itself and
Likewise the sixteenth [are extracted] by the adept.

That which is the first of the third
And likewise the twenty-sixth,
That which is the third of the fourth and
The second sibilant.[20]
That which is the first of the first
And thus the twenty-seventh.
Again the twenty-eighth,
The third of the first,
The fourth of the fifth as well.
Likewise take the thirty-first
As well as the fifteenth itself.
Likewise the twenty-fifth
And that which is the second of the first.
Likewise the twenty-sixth and
The thirty-second letter.

---

20. The term "sibilant" was taken from David Gray's translation.

The last of the sibilants,
And again the thirty-second.
The fourth of the fifth and
The third of the second.
The fourth of the fifth and
The third sibilant,
Again the twenty-seventh
And the first semivowel.
Likewise the twenty-first again
And the second semivowel.
Likewise the thirtieth again
And the first of the fifth.

Also, the first sibilant and
Likewise the letter DYA as well.
That which is the first of the fourth
And that which is the first sibilant.
Likewise the twenty-eighth
And that which is the second of the first.
The first of the third as well, and
That which is the third of the first.
That which is the fourth of the fourth,
And the second semivowel.
The fifth of the third as well.
Then the BYA is taken.
The fourth of the first
Then the eighth itself as well.
That which is the fifth of the fourth,
The fifth of the fifth as well.
Likewise the twenty-seventh,
The fourth of the fourth,
Again the twenty-seventh,
Likewise the twenty-sixth.
The twenty-fifth is correctly extracted,
The thirty-third as well.
The fourth of the fourth and

The fifth of the fifth.
The fifth of the fourth as well,
And the first of the first itself.
Likewise the twenty-seventh,
The fourth semivowel as well.
Likewise the twenty-first,
The second sibilant itself,
Likewise the twenty-sixth.

The secret mantra of the *King of Knowledge*
Accomplishes all activities.
There is nothing more supreme
Than this in the three worlds.

By knowing the mantra of glorious Heruka
Other [mantras] are like dry grass compared to fire.
This is the famous root mantra.

FROM THE SPEECH OF GLORIOUS HERUKA, "THE RITUAL OF COLLECTING THE LETTERS OF THE ROOT MANTRA" IS THE FIFTH CHAPTER.

6. The Armor of the Six Heroes

Furthermore there are the twenty-two syllables
And the seven syllables of the essence and close essence [mantras].
There is the seed of the eighth of the YA collection,
Likewise [adorned] by the twelve ornaments.
By taking out the letters between
[You obtain] the six branches spoken by Heruka.

Attached to the six heroes
Abiding perfectly in each letter
And perfectly endowed with
OM NAMA SÖHA BOKAT
HUM HUM PHAT.
The essence should be known by the practitioner.

The first is at the heart itself,
Know the second at the head,
The third correctly placed on the crown of the head,
The fourth is the armor itself,
The fifth is at the eyes,
And the sixth is said to be a weapon.[21]

FROM THE SPEECH OF GLORIOUS HERUKA, "THE ARMOR OF
THE SIX HEROES" IS THE SIXTH CHAPTER.

---

21. This signifies placing the armor mantras at the various parts of the body.

7. The Condensed Rituals of the Root Mantra

And then the thirteenth vowel itself
Is joined with the second syllable.
The eleventh vowel is perfectly
Adorned by the sixth syllable.
Also the fourth vowel is
Attached to the seventh syllable itself.
The eleventh vowel
Is skillfully attached to the eighth syllable.
The ninth syllable is adorned
With the second vowel.
The second vowel itself is attached to
The twelfth syllable.
Taking the twenty-first letter
Possessing the second vowel,
The adept then joins them to the fourteenth syllable.
Taking the twentieth letter
And combining it with the third vowel, then
Combine them with the fifteenth syllable.
The fifteenth of the vowels is perfectly endowed with
The beautiful sixteenth syllable.
The third vowel is endowed with
The seventeenth syllable, which is combined [with it].
The second vowel is
Attached to the eighteenth syllable.
The second vowel is
Attached to the twenty-first syllable.

The fifth vowel is
Attached to the twenty-third syllable.
The thirteenth vowel is
Attached to the twenty-fourth syllable.
Having extracted the first group [of written letters]
Attach it to the twenty-fifth syllable.
The twenty-sixth syllable should be
Endowed with the second vowel.
The twenty-eighth is also
Attached to the fifteenth vowel.
The twenty-ninth syllable is
Perfectly endowed with the first of the third,
The part below endowed with fire,
And likewise attach the second vowel.

The thirty-first syllable is
Attached to the second vowel.
The thirty-second is
Attached to the thirteenth vowel.
The thirty-third syllable should be
Correctly endowed with the sun.
The fourth vowel endowed with
The thirty-fourth syllable
Will accomplish all your desired aims.
The fifth vowel itself,
Perfectly endowed with the thirty-seventh,
Accomplishes the dakinis.
As for the thirty-eighth,
Attach it to the second vowel.
Have no doubt this will
Accomplish all the deities.

The forty-second is likewise
Attached by the practitioner to fire.
The forty-third syllable

Is attached to the fifth vowel.
The forty-fifth is also
Attached to the second vowel.
The fifth vowel is also
Endowed with the forty-sixth.
This is the excellent, supreme offering of all the heroes.
The forty-seventh is itself
Attached to the second vowel.
This is the supreme Vajrasattva.

The fifty-first is made
Supremely beautiful by combining it
With the fifth vowel.
The fifty-second itself is
Attached to the second vowel.
Have no doubt this is the way
To accomplish all deities.
The fifty-third syllable is
Attached to the thirteenth vowel.
The fifty-sixth syllable is
Correctly attached to the sixth vowel—
With it enemies are definitely destroyed.
The fourth semivowel is
Attached to the second vowel, and
Likewise, by attaching the fifteenth [vowel]
To the fifty-ninth syllable,
All realizations will be attained.
The sixty-first syllable is
Perfectly endowed with the second vowel.
This is explained to be supreme.
The sixty-second syllable is
Attached to the third vowel,
The supreme desire of the dakinis.
The sixty-third syllable is also
Perfectly endowed with the eleventh vowel,
The most beautiful supreme syllable.

Likewise the sixty-fifth
Is split apart by Vajrasattva.
This seed is the supreme substance of the gods.
The greatest gift is to bestow liberation.
The sixty-sixth syllable is
Correctly attached to the third vowel and
Bestows attainment of all actions
According to the speech of the tathagatas.
The sixty-seventh syllable is
Perfectly endowed with the second vowel.
Have no doubt that all of these are
The deeds of the yogini!
The sixty-eighth as well is
Attached to the letter *b*.

Take this seed syllable
And set it in the lower portion.

The seventy-first syllable
Is perfectly endowed with the second vowel.
Have no doubt that there is beauty
In all these letters!
Correctly attaching the second vowel to
The seventy-fourth itself, it
Is primordially accomplished
As the Tathagata taught.
The seventy-fifth letter is
Endowed with the sixth vowel.
This, the excellent, supreme yoga
Is supreme of all actions.
The seventy-sixth is also
Endowed with the second vowel,
Split by the sun, and
Attached to the letter *v*.
There exists no other more supremely beautiful
Than this.

Attach the seventy-seventh syllable
To DHA.
The beautiful dakinis believe
This seed [syllable] is the supreme substance.
The seventy-eighth is
Endowed with the second vowel.
This seed [syllable] is the very best
And believed to be the supreme cause.

The eighty-first syllable,
Distinguished with the [vowel] after the fourth,
Is primordially accomplished.
The eighty-second syllable
Attached to the two vowels[22]
Engages all the attainments.

By extracting [these letters] from the diagram
Of the protector, glorious Heruka,
Understand the supreme root mantra.

It is the abode of all attainments
And destroys the hearts of the dakinis.
By reciting the [mantra] of the glorious *Drinker of Blood*,
The *King of Wisdom Deities*, [you] will accomplish your aims.

Attaching the syllable OM at the beginning
And HUM HUM PHAT at the end,
This mantra is the root mantra
That bestows all attainments.

FROM THE SPEECH OF GLORIOUS HERUKA, "THE CONDENSED
RITUALS OF THE ROOT MANTRA" IS THE SEVENTH CHAPTER.

---

22. There are two pages of extra text dealing with the mantra in the sTog Palace edition of the
tantra that are not in the Phugdrag edition. See also Gray 2007, 192n20.

8. The Essence of the Reversed Armor and the Ritual of the Condensed Mantra of the Six Dakinis

Next, the nature of oneself
Is unified with all heroes:
Heruka Chakrasamvara is asserted
To be the net [binding] the dakinis.

HA SÖ RAM BA SHAM LA DZA NI KI DA PHAT
HUM HUM KAM RU RU HE HE VAJRA SHRI OM

This is the essence of the *King of Knowledge*
That has not arisen nor will arise.

PHAT HUM HUM HA HA HRIH OM

The syllables BAM and OM,
The syllables MOM and HRIM,
And HUM and PHAT, are enumerated.
These are explained as the six yoginis.[23]

OM VAJRA BEROTZANIYE SÖHA[24]

The great knowledge of the dakinis
Has not arisen nor will arise.

---

23. This is in reference to the armor deities of the mother.
24. For some reason this mantra is not written in reverse in the Tibetan text.

On this earth there are the four precious [mantras].
This is the sacred mantra rosary.
The great knowledge of the dakinis is
Heruka, the *King of Knowledge*.

FROM THE SPEECH OF GLORIOUS HERUKA, "THE ESSENCE
OF THE REVERSED ARMOR AND THE RITUAL OF THE
CONDENSED MANTRA OF THE SIX DAKINIS" IS THE EIGHTH
CHAPTER.

9. The Ritual Actions of the Root Mantra

NEXT, THE STAGES of the supreme actions of the root secret mantra are explained. Whatever exists in the three worlds is accomplished in an instant and all actions are performed. All the gods and all the nagas and all the givers of harm (*yakshas*) and smell-eaters (*gandharvas*), in all of the places where they live, by merely remembering it [the root mantra] once, will be killed. All the clouds will disperse, the rain will descend and reverse, and the oceans will dry up. The rivers will change direction and then descend. It can impede Indra. By reciting this secret mantra one hundred thousand times, the earth quakes, you can climb trees, and wherever you wish to go you can go. It captures all mantras and all realizations. It causes blood to flow out and then flow back in again. You can transform into a hundred thousand forms. If you wish you can appear and if you wish you can disappear. The mansion, treetops, and so forth are transformed to dust. You can make poison into nectar and nectar into poison. You can make the moon into water and make the water into the moon. You can capture all scents. You can travel anywhere you desire, like a garuda. Collecting all peaceful goddesses for the supreme person who is engaged in all actions, the power that exists in the palm of your hand cannot be stolen by anyone. Possessing such a ritual will accomplish the fruits of all attainments.

By merely remembering you can kill or generate fire. You can go beneath the ground and cause hail to fall or drive it away. By merely remembering this mantra, lightning will strike and cause the reflections of all deities to dance. If you recite this mantra once while holding the name of someone, in an instant he will die. You will come to enjoy all the spiritual grounds you desire and assemble all wishes. With this Bhagavan [Heruka] you do not need to observe a special way of acting and you don't need to fast. Through this ritual of reflection, engage in whatever actions you desire.

If it is recited wrathfully once, ten million will be killed. If you recite it peacefully it will [give] life. By reciting it once in the burning charnel grounds, if one strikes someone they will instantly fall. Recite it completely in the ashes [of the charnel grounds]; whomever one strikes, in that instant the flesheaters (*pishachas*) will seize them. Write a person's full name on a plank and so forth at night, and if you recite it once in the burning charnel grounds, they will be seized by a planetary spirit.[25] By reciting once on the twig of a poplar tree, whomever one strikes [with it], by the power of the wind they will come. Having recited it once on a pebble, whoever touches it will become stiff with fright and go wherever you wish. Burn *gugul* incense[26] and recite [the mantra] once and then if you [burn] the incense the [spirits] will possess all sentient beings. Recite it once on your hand, and then if you place that hand on someone who was bitten by a black poisonous snake, that person will be healed. By reciting the dakinis' seal once on water, that water can destroy whatever you place it upon. By reciting it once on a twig of the *karavira* tree you can transfer to the womb of whomever you wish.

This is the secret mantra of the glorious *Drinker of Blood*. If one does not know this [practice] yet sincerely desires the attainments, that one will get only the chaff; if one does not possess this secret mantra one will obtain neither attainments nor bliss. For one who does not know this secret mantra yet sincerely wishes to be a yogi, hard work is useless and [he] will not obtain the results.

This secret mantra bestows all the attainments for one who enjoys desire; the practitioner of the mantra and mudra is knowledgeable of this teaching of the Sugata: that food, drink, and the other offerings, and the tastes of food, drink, and so forth, will be obtained. By this excellent offering you will receive all the attainments.

FROM THE SPEECH OF GLORIOUS HERUKA, "THE RITUAL ACTIONS OF THE ROOT MANTRA" IS THE NINTH CHAPTER.

25. This term refers to Rahu, the spirit that consumes the sun or moon during eclipses.
26. Skt. *guggula;* Gray (2007, 200) says this is bdellium.

10. Accomplishing the Three Bodies and the Ritual of the Essence Mantra

And then, the explanation of the three bodies
Through the nondual union with the *Drinker of Blood*,
By merely knowing which
There will be attainments;
Of this you should have no doubt.

When one becomes a practitioner
Endowed with the body of the dharmakaya,
Thus perfectly transforming the mind,
At such a time I proclaim exalted wisdom.

When one becomes a practitioner
Endowed with the body of the sambogakaya
And in meditative equipoise,
At such a time I proclaim complete enjoyment.

When one becomes a practitioner
Endowed with the body of the nirmanakaya
And the mind single-pointed,
At such a time I proclaim the emanation body.

Without a doubt you will perfectly obtain
The exalted wisdom, complete enjoyment, and emanation [bodies].
Have no doubt that you will
Receive this attainment of Shri Heruka.

This is the essence of secret mantra.

The practitioner should listen to the explanation of these secrets:

Through reciting the essence [mantra], you can come and go ten million miles and become a superior being. You can transform into many thousands of forms, or ascend to the top of a mansion, tree, or house and [travel] together with the yoginis many thousands of miles away, coming and going in no other way than through the sky.

If you wish you will quickly appear and if you wish you will disappear. If you wish to become young, middle aged, or old, you will obtain such forms.

If you wish to become an elephant, water buffalo, wild ox, tiger, lion, bull, cat, rabbit, or camel, you will obtain such forms. If you wish to become a peacock, cock, goose, red wild duck, water fowl, owl, hawk, vulture, or crow, you will obtain such forms. Whatever you wish to become, you will obtain such forms. You can capture words, capture sights, capture sounds, capture scents, and capture tastes. According to your desires you can drain someone's blood or make them stiff.

FROM THE SPEECH OF GLORIOUS HERUKA, "ACCOMPLISHING THE THREE BODIES AND THE RITUAL OF THE ESSENCE MANTRA" IS THE TENTH CHAPTER.

11. The Ritual of the Characteristics of the Seven-Birthed One

Furthermore, these things will occur:
By merely relying [on this practice]
The practitioner will be born seven times [as a human].
And it is taught that you will quickly induce the attainments
And accomplish all realizations.

The person from whom a sweet scent of perspiration arises, who speaks the truth and has not closed his eyes for a long time, who does not become angry, and whose breath is very delicious, is a person who has taken a human rebirth seven times. His manner of walking is without the seven defilements and he is endowed with flawless compassion.

In dependence upon such a person, extracting his heart and reciting the essence mantra of glorious Heruka one hundred and eight times and forming a drop, you will fly, traveling ten million miles. By merely relying on that you will quickly come to possess the exalted wisdom of the three worlds. You will travel back and forth five million miles in one day and one night. You will attain the body of the deity, what is known to be the essence of Heruka. Whatever one desires will be bestowed.

FROM THE SPEECH OF GLORIOUS HERUKA, "THE RITUAL OF THE CHARACTERISTICS OF THE SEVEN-BIRTHED ONE" IS THE ELEVENTH CHAPTER.

12. The Ritual of the Close Essence Mantra

Next, the close essence [mantra]:
It is taught that all the attainments will be obtained and
Everything in all the three worlds
Will be accomplished in an instant.

PHAT HUM HUM HA HA HRIH OM

This is the heart of the close essence [mantra].

If you recite this mantra one hundred thousand times, the earth will quake in all three worlds. Gods and demigods, givers of harm, cannibals (*rakshasas*), nagas, smell-eaters, centaurs (*kimnaras*), or anything else will be summoned.

Oceans, waterfalls, ponds, and so forth can be dried up or taken under control. All the dakinis will serve the practitioner in the place where you recite [this mantra]. By reciting the mantra in that manner, if you wash your own eyes you will gain knowledge of those born as a human seven times; those whose life is exhausted will appear as if dead, and those with a long life will appear with vitality. By reciting the mantra on the eyes, whomever one sees will be suppressed. Take the skin off the soles of the feet of a dead hero and place human blood, ground-up ear, and eye medicine together in a skullcup. Mix antimony, *giwang*,[27] saffron, and blood together and dry it in the shade wrapped in the three metals to keep it nicely. Prepare it during the month of Gyalda.[28]

27. A medicine made from the liver of various animals.
28. The special month of Heruka and Vajrayogini, beginning on the sixteenth day of the eleventh month and lasting until the fifteenth day of the twelfth month of the lunar calendar.

Put it in the mouth of [yourself as] glorious Heruka and cover your mouth with your left hand. Then, if you recite [the mantra] one hundred and eight times in the following moment, you will become invisible and your shadow will disappear and not even the gods will be able to see you. What need is there to mention, then, that people on earth will be unable to see you? Remove it again from your mouth and you will become visible. In this tantra this is the pill attainment of "enjoying the sky" that was taught by the hero himself.

With these mantras—the essence and close essence mantras of glorious Heruka—if you rub the tip of your finger on a fleshless skull, blood will be drawn forth. Rub the skull with the left [finger] again and again, and the blood will reenter. If you press on the skull while reciting clearly, whoever's name you say, the brain of that person will become ill. With subsequent mindfulness of the secret mantra, fill the skullcup with milk and that one will [again] become well. If you recite [the mantra] over *giwang* medicine and form a drop, whoever sees that drop will be bound. By reciting [the mantra] over the finger, anyone to whom a threatening mudra is then shown will quickly fall down. When reciting the mantra, press your feet on the ground while saying [their] name and they will die. Recite it in water, then throw the water on the ground and that one will come back to life. Recite this mantra a thousand times or more with fingers pointed, and if accompanied by a threatening mudra, everything you see will quickly be subjugated and, with a word, will again be released.

Reciting these one hundred times in the ashes of a butcher, afterward whichever form one thinks of, by striking a sentient being they will quickly take on that form. Reciting these one hundred times in the ashes of a burned offering, even the gods themselves cannot see whom you strike. If you recite [this mantra] one hundred times in water and then toss it [on him] he will again become visible.

Sealing and binding a skullcup shut, without breathing, recite their name and they will quickly become insane and a thousand other beings will become insane as well. You can mentally release them by reciting their name. Taking the hair from the crown of your head, recite ten times and tie it in a knot, and all the dakinis will come. Going to an empty house, recite one hundred times and bind your hair to the top of your head. Open your eyes and as long as you recite the [mantra], you will remain invisible. If you untie your hair, [you] will reappear. Recite [the mantra] perfectly in a skullcup and then if you throw it above, below, or in the cardinal and intermediate directions, gods, demigods, yakshas, cannibals, and smell-eaters, as well as centaurs and serpent spirits (*mahoragas*), will all be bound. You can steal all the dakinis' yogas. By seeing a woman and man in bed, if you recite the mantra they will be [forever] joined and united. If you recite the mantra one hundred and eight times you will quickly be able to release them and they will be liberated by your mind.

If you recite [the mantra] together with gravel in a skullcup and then enter a river, [it will] cause it to flow upstream and then descend. The skullcup will quickly suppress the waves, which will be overcome by the mind. Recite the mantra and look upward in accordance with the view of emptiness and a great rain will quickly stop. With a host of others coming from all directions recite [the mantra] one thousand times and when battle is engaged if they strike you with weapons, not only will you not be injured but the weapons will not cut [you] and you will [come to] possess the vajra body.

FROM THE SPEECH OF GLORIOUS HERUKA, "THE RITUAL OF THE CLOSE ESSENCE MANTRA" IS THE TWELFTH CHAPTER.

13. The Ritual of the Armor Mantra

Next, the actions of the armor:
Whatever there is in the three worlds
And everything the mind desires [will be obtained].
This will be explained according to their sequence.

If you recite the armor [mantras] while on the path, you will not be frightened by either a thief or a tiger, or you will become invisible. Recite the armor [mantra] while you are entering the abode of the women of the king's palace and you will become invisible. Taking that which you desire and then leaving, even the gods will not be able to see [you]. Recite the armor mantra one hundred times and whomever you touch with your hand, while touching them, they will become paralyzed. Even the thirty-three [gods] will not [be able] to move [him]. If you press on [him] with your foot and recite [the mantra] he will be released. Draw your own blood and recite [the mantra] three times, and anyone with whom you speak, and whoever sees you, or whom you see, will all have their blood drawn.

By reciting [the mantra] one thousand times wrathfully in someone's house, they will quickly come down with an infectious disease. If you take water and recite [the mantra over it] five times and then sprinkle it, they will recover. Whomever's face you see [while] reciting [the mantra], his words will be stolen. If you recite the mantra one thousand times at the banks of a river, you will be able to walk on top of that water as if it were solid. In that manner you can go across [any body of] water. If you enter the water, you can remain within rivers as well as the ocean.

If you rub your two hands [together] and recite [the mantra] one thousand times, the yoginis will be subjugated. The yoginis who have a variety of forms, such as Dakini, Lama, Khandaroha, and Rupini, are all well known; they will serve the yogi and all of them will be subjugated.

By preparing cloth during the lunar conjunction with the Gyal (Pushya) mansion[29] and wearing it on your body while engaging in meditative equipoise on the yoginis, if you recite [the mantra] ten thousand times you will accomplish [the attainment of] going underground. If you wear this on your body you will become invisible in space for up to one thousand miles. Wherever you wish to go you can go. Whether to the ends of the earth or upon the ocean you can immediately go.

One will move the stream [of bodhichitta] upward. That nature of whatever appears to the path of the senses is all transformed into buddhas through the supreme mental stabilization of union.

Extract the sap from a coral tree[30] and recite [the mantra] one thousand times. On whomever the drop [falls] that one will become a tree. By reciting [the mantra] in some water seven times and then throwing it [at them] they will again be restored. Taking the dust from the bottom of an elephant's foot and saying the recitation one thousand times, whomever you strike will turn into an elephant.

FROM THE SPEECH OF GLORIOUS HERUKA, "THE RITUAL OF THE ARMOR MANTRA" IS THE THIRTEENTH CHAPTER.

29. That is, while the moon is in the mansion of Gyal (Skt. Pushya); see note 28.
30. Skt. *parijata;* I obtained the identification of this tree from Gray (2007, 215).

14. Engaging in the Donkey Ritual

Next, the explanation of the sadhana:
The self-yoga for attaining the aspect of a donkey
By which the attainments are accomplished
In order to reverse the activity of the mind.

The dakinis such as Dakini, Lama,
Khandaroha, and Rupini,
Are in the aspect of a donkey with blood on their faces
And holding a three-pointed [spear] in their hands.

If you accomplish [them] you can see the
Length of your life and its completion.
This is the yoga of the donkey.
Likewise see yourself as you
Were before, as a donkey
Or even an elephant.

Seeing the form of an elephant,
The yogi perceives the various aspects of his former lives,
Where he was born, as what, and such.

If a treasure-like practitioner
Born as a man for seven previous lives
Makes a torma and offers it,
He will achieve spiritual attainments.

Through this you can travel
One hundred miles or even a thousand.

This is the principal, supreme mantra yoga
That accomplishes the union of the dakinis.
The one who recites with the sign of the yogini
Will accomplish this in one month.
This is the secret tantra,
The virtuous essence of the mantra.

The yogi who knows this supreme suchness
Should be without doubts.
It is proclaimed that these make up the
Net that binds the dakinis.

FROM THE SPEECH OF GLORIOUS HERUKA, "ENGAGING IN THE DONKEY RITUAL" IS THE FOURTEENTH CHAPTER.

15. The Ritual of the Signs of Each One of the Syllables

Next, all the vows:
Have no doubt that
He who knows the signs will
Achieve accomplishments by means of suchness.

Thus *DA* is said to be "person."
Thus *DI* is "woman."
Thus *BU* is "to subdue."
Thus *SU* is "eating."
Thus *MA* is said to be "mother."
Thus *YO* is "wife."
Thus *BHI* is likewise "sister."
Thus *BI* is said to be "girlfriend."
Thus *LU* is "daughter."
Thus *STRI* should be known as "blood."
Thus *SO* is "drinking soma."[31]
Thus *BE* is likewise "drink."
Thus *HI* is likewise said to be "flesh."
Thus *BHA* is said to be "eating."
Thus *BHU* is said to be "meeting place."
Thus *BI* is likewise a "charnel ground."
Thus *DHU* is known as "corpse."
Thus *DHI* is said to be the "yogini."
Thus *GA* is therefore "Lama."

---

31. Thanks to David Gray for the word *soma*.

Thus *TRI* is said to be "Rupini."

Thus *KU* is likewise "Dakini."

Thus *HA* is "Khandaroha" herself.

Thus *JA* is the "two calves."

Thus *KA* is a "pair of arms."

Thus *BHA* is "speaking sincerely."

Thus *SU* is a "friendly welcome."

Thus *MI* is a "fish."

Thus *BA* is "eating."

Thus *BE* is "drinkable."

Thus *GHA* is to "traverse or not to traverse."

Thus *KA* is "desire."

Thus *SA* is "should not go to another."

Thus *RA* is a "widow."

Thus *DU* is known as a "woman of bad character."

Thus *SU* is "fortunate woman."

Thus *NA* is "unfortunate woman."

Thus *SA* is "endowed with commitments."

Thus *A* is "without commitments."

Thus *AH* is "coming."

Thus *NA* is "not coming."

Thus *SO* is "attachment."

Each one of these letters is a sign and known by the hero and the sisters as offering respect and disrespect. They are beneficial to the one endowed with supreme commitments and should be offered to those who act with respect.

FROM THE SPEECH OF GLORIOUS HERUKA, "THE RITUAL OF THE SIGNS OF EACH ONE OF THE SYLLABLES" IS THE FIFTEENTH CHAPTER.

16. Examining the Characteristics of the Seven Yoginis

Next, I shall briefly explain
The fortunate and unfortunate:
Offer perfect respect to those who
Abide in the supreme commitments and
Are fortunate, beneficial, and pleasing agents.

Next is the distinction of the spiritual family:
The yogini who is nondual with the hero
Whom by merely knowing
The practitioner obtains the spiritual attainments.

A woman like the full white lotus root
With elongated eyes like a lotus petal,
Always gayly dressed in white,
Possessing the scent of fresh sandalwood,
And delighting in the assembly of the sugatas,
Should be known as one born into the spiritual family.

The woman who is like refined gold,
Delights in wearing red and gold,
And is endowed with the scent of jasmine and *champa* flower,
As such is a follower of the hero.

Whoever is like the pale-green *utpala* flower,
Delights in maintaining blue-colored clothing,
And has the scent of a blue utpala flower,
This one is a follower of the hero.

The beautiful woman with
Skin like the petals of a white lotus,
Who always smells like the root of a lotus,
Is thus in the thoughts of the hero.

Whichever woman is of white and red,
With a good form and wearing red,
With the scent of jasmine and utpala,
She is a manifestation of the vajra lineage.

Whichever woman is of yellow and green,
Delights in wearing white clothes,
Whose head is endowed with the scent of a flower,
Is thus a follower of the tathagata lineage.

Whichever woman is red in color,
Wearing clothes of the same and
Always bearing the scent of camphor,
Is thus a follower of the Vairochana lineage.

These are the spiritual families of yoginis.
Thus they are definitely explained as seven in number.
Always joyfully performing everything with the left,
They have their own colors and signs.

The knowledge letters of the lineage as well as
The followers of the lineage
Have six colors.

Each bound by their own mudra and
Speaking the words of her own spiritual family,
Any woman who goes to the left is
Always to the left of the yoginis as well.
Her speech is the great, excellent proclamation.
Looking to the left is her way of looking.

[When] seeing these women one should speak [with them].
This is explained as being endowed with commitments.

While making requests of all such women,
Speak with the seed syllables of their lineage,
Without discarding the actions of their lineage, and
Maintain the teachings of their own scriptures.

Reciting the knowledge [mantra] of their own lineage,
One is said to be "endowed with the commitments."
When prostrating one should always
Incline the body to the left.

One should speak with the goddesses,
Always moving toward the definitive truth.

[Dig] into the earth with the big toe
And draw the lines with the foot,
Scratch one's head with the left hand and
Look from out the corner of your eye.

The practitioner should especially
Remain mindful of one's knowledge [goddess],
Pointing at the cheek, the neck,
And the nostril, with one's finger.

Look sideways toward the
Knowledge [goddess] and recite the mantra once.
The yogini who moves toward the truth is
Perfectly endowed with the commitments.

FROM THE SPEECH OF GLORIOUS HERUKA, "EXAMINING
THE CHARACTERISTICS OF THE [SEVEN] YOGINIS" IS THE
SIXTEENTH CHAPTER.

17. The Ritual of All the Dakinis' Forms, Hand Symbols, and Teaching the Mudra

Next, the difficulty of finding the yoginis,
And likewise the dakinis, being
The perfect source of the five nectars.

Yamini (Yamini), Trak Chema (Trasani),
Naktsalma (Kanani), Deshin Jik (Bhima),
Beautiful Suk (Rupa) and Kunchöma (Samcara), and
Bhasura (Bhasura) are the seven dakinis.[32]

Here is a brief explanation of their characteristics:
Rupini (Rupika), Tsumbika (Chumbika),
Lama (Lama), Yongyur (Paravritta), Jichemo (Sabalika),
Midok (Anivartika), and Ehika Lhamo (Aihikidevi),
Are explained as the seven dakinis.

First she looks with passion,
Then she wrinkles her eyebrows.
First she assumes a form,
Then subsequently destroys it.
This one should be known as Rupini
Who is explained as nondual with the hero.

Whether it is wished for or not
She embraces and kisses a child.

32. Thanks to David Gray for the Sanskrit names of these seven dakinis.

She should be known as Tsumbika;
This dakini is the destroyer of nonvirtue.

The one who looks from the corner [of her eye]
With wrathful wrinkles,
A threatening mudra and a raised eyebrow,
Who breathes with a ferocious manner
Not breathing as well,
Who acts in a terrifying manner,
She is said to be Lama.

A pig, a red bear, or a cat,
A goat, jackal, hunter, or horse,
She who terrifies them all
Is the one said to be Yongyur.

Because of [her] great joy [she] laughs
And once gone does not return again,
Openly lustful and clearly passionate,
She is said to be Khandaroha.

[She] is anxious and if she touches you
With her hand, a lump of earth,
Her foot, the fray of her clothing,
Or a tree, you will not live.
She is known as Midokpa
And is proclaimed as the one not to be accomplished.

[She] who laughs, speaks without reason,
Weeps, or gets very angry,
She is remembered as Ehika.
She is a goddess who speaks sincerely
And always speaks with Buddhists,
And has arisen from a vajra lineage.

These are the mudras of the dakini lineage
Who, for the sake of teaching the hero, use weapons:
A skull, an ax, bared fangs,
A wheel, armor, a victory banner,
A sword terrifying to all, and
A conch shell are known as the eight [weapons].

These are explained as the mudras of the lineage.

FROM THE SPEECH OF GLORIOUS HERUKA, "THE RITUAL OF ALL THE DAKINIS' FORMS, HAND SYMBOLS, AND TEACHING THE MUDRA" IS THE SEVENTEENTH CHAPTER.

18. The Definitive Ritual of the Signs, Characteristics, and Colors of All the Dakinis

Next, further explanations:
The supreme state of the dakinis,
Through which one perfectly understands the dakinis
[Who] abide by the commitments.

Any woman of red and gold,
Exuding the smell of a lotus,
Whose nature of looking and walking is peaceful,
Is followed by an affectionate glance.

Any woman who has red fingernails
As well as love for all beings,
With drawings of lotuses in her house,
That one is in the lineage of Padmanarteshvara.

A trident between her eyebrows,
Her body of gray and blue,
Always meditating on the vajra lineage,
Her house has drawings of a vajra.

The one who always makes offerings
Is the glorious dakini;
There is no doubt that she is a dakini
Arisen from the lineage of Heruka.

On her forehead is a trident and
What looks like a small spear;
Her eyes are red and orange
And her legs and hands are red.

Toward goats and hens
Her mind is always joyous.
She has drawings of a vajra in her house and
Always makes offerings to them.
Have no doubt that this dakini
Has arisen from the lineage of Shri Heruka.

On her forehead is a wheel,
Which appears on her hand as well,
Dark as a raincloud.
With silk always bound on her forehead,
She has great fortune and excellence,
Full of supreme bliss, with
A drawing of a wheel in her house
To which she always makes offerings:
This one has arisen from the lineage of Vajravarahi.

This dakini is proud of her power,
The one with black eyebrows and
White buck teeth,
Always vicious and [uses her] left,
Endowed with courage,
She ever delights in bathing and
Mostly keeps silent.

With a drawing of a vajra in [her] house
To which she always makes virtuous offerings,
Arisen from the lineage of Vajravarahi,
She is endowed with fifteen thousand [in her retinue].

Appearing in colors like yellow and gold,
Her eyes unmoving with a yellow mustache,
On her forehead appears a vajra,
On her hand as well.
She ever abides in kingdoms,
With great pride proclaiming the truth,
Exuding the scent of jasmine,
With a vajra in her house,
To which she is always making beautiful offerings,
[She] has arisen from the lineage of Khandaroha.

This supremely powerful dakini
Always delights in flesh.
She is thin and black with red eyes.
Her forehead has a sign like a three-pointed spear
And delights in bad actions.

Always going to the charnel grounds,
Neither afraid nor dirty,
On her forehead is a drop.
A skull is drawn in her house and
To that she makes offerings.
She has arisen from a lineage of the
dakini of glorious Heruka.

Any woman whose color is like a cloud,
Whose teeth are uneven and
Who delights in mischievous actions,
Showing bared teeth on the left,
With an ax drawn in her house
To which she ever makes offerings,
Have no doubt she is a dakini
Arising from the lineage of Vinayaka.

This collection of dakinis
Arose from the lineage of Shri Heruka

To benefit practitioners.
These are emanations with secret characteristics.

FROM THE SPEECH OF GLORIOUS HERUKA, "THE DEFINITIVE RITUAL OF THE SIGNS, CHARACTERISTICS, AND COLORS OF ALL THE DAKINIS" IS THE EIGHTEENTH CHAPTER.

19. Showing All the Mudras and Reply Mudras of the Yoginis

Next, the excellent explanation
By which the practitioner can recognize
The physical characteristics of [the dakini] Lama.

With a wide face that is
Perfectly round in appearance,
Her chin always has a beard.
She is decorated with long eyebrows,
Has fine clothes, is clean and peaceful,
Unagitated and speaks the truth,
[She] always delights in the holy Dharma.
She is explained to be the sister of the hero.

Offer the lotus mudra
Or engage in the turtle mudra,
An antelope-skin [mudra] or a water-vessel [mudra]
Are said to be her reply mudra.

Her time is the tenth day [of the month]
And she has a drawing of a lotus in her house.
Women with these characteristics
Are [the dakini] Lama.

With two moist lips and elongated eyes
That remain red and pale yellow,
Wealthy and fortunate, with glorious good qualities

And a yellow appearance like a champa [flower],
Neither too tall nor too short,
[She] delights in a variety of garments.
On her forehead there are three lines
Moving upward toward her hairline;
She laughs joyously,
Subduing the path and dwelling [there].
She always delights in stories
Of death and battle.

Thus when seeing this proud woman
Show [her] the spear mudra,
Draw up your left leg
And display a dance;
Turning perfectly to the left
Is said to be [her] reply mudra.

The fourteenth and the eighth day
Are said to be her allotted times,
And there is a drawing of the trident in her house
To which she continuously makes offerings.
These are the characteristics of
Lama, *Powerful One of the World.*

She has perfect cheeks
And luminous pores,
Likewise always red and yellow.
Her eyes always appear greenish-yellow,
Her hair is in whirls,
Her head and forehead are bound by silk
And [there] is a single perfect line.
Likewise her neck is long and she
Always delights in wearing red.
Laughing and singing are the very reply.

Suddenly becoming wrathful,
Her mind agitated,

She delights in arguments.
Looking at such a proud [dakini],
Offer [her] the spear mudra,
Then offer the bell mudra.
Turning to the left
Is said to be [her] reply mudra.

Her calves are short and round and she
Always delights in wearing yellow garments.
Her garments hang down over her shoulders.
When seeing such a woman
Show the wheel mudra.
Secondly, try hard to
Show the spear mudra.
Turning perfectly to the left
Is said to be [her] reply mudra.

The fourteenth [day of the month] is her time.
She has a drawing of a vajra in her house.
These are characteristics of
[The dakini] Lama of Shri Heruka.

Her entire body has small hairs and
Her eyes are black and yellow.
She is thick and awful,
With a huge face and a large mouth,
A round belly, and black in color;
With round eyes and a damaged nose,
Ever adept at singing and charming,
She is the color of a cloud.

When seeing one who is proud in this way
Display the naga mudra.
Secondly, try hard as well
To show her the spear mudra.
Turning completely to the left
Is said to be [her] reply mudra,

The eleventh [day of the month] is her time.
With a drawing of fangs in her house,
These are the characteristics of
Vajravarahi Lama.

FROM THE SPEECH OF GLORIOUS HERUKA, "SHOWING ALL
THE MUDRAS AND REPLY MUDRAS OF THE YOGINIS" IS THE
NINETEENTH CHAPTER.

20. The Ritual of Signs and Mudras of All the Yoginis

Next, I will explain further
The signs of the left hand
By which you will understand
Perfectly who are brothers and sisters.

Whoever shows the left hand
Is saying "I speak truthfully."

Whoever shows the ring finger
Is responding "[I am] speaking truthfully."

Whoever slaps their stomach
Is saying "We are hungry."

Whoever shows their forehead
Is saying "I arrived from the sky."

Whoever puts their finger in their mouth
Is saying "I am eating."

Whoever moves their tongue
Is saying "I have eaten."

Whoever touches their knee
Is saying "I am exhausted."

Whoever touches the tip of their finger
Is saying "I have slept."

Whoever gnashes their teeth
Is saying "I am eating flesh."

Whoever displays a wrathful expression
Is saying "I am bound."

Whoever shows a garuda [mudra]
Is saying "I am liberated."

Whoever shows a clenched fist,
Show her a trident [in response].

Look with a sidelong expression
At whoever shows their hair,
And show her the khatvanga staff.
To whoever moves their limbs,
Show the two bared fangs.

Whoever shows one hand with [the other] hand,
Is thus saying "The torma should be eaten."

Whoever shows the right hand
Is saying "Do it this way."

Whoever touches their ear
Is saying "You should stay."

Whoever touches one fingernail with the other
Is saying "Carry the corpse."

Whoever draws on the earth
Is saying "Today I will enter the mandala."

Whoever touches the breast
Is saying "Protect my child."

Whoever draws with the left thumb
Is saying "The guru protects living beings."

Whoever opens their eyes
Is saying "Act this way."

Whoever touches the knuckles
Is saying "Blissful sleep."

All of these should be displayed
To whomever is suitable to be a messenger.

FROM THE SPEECH OF GLORIOUS HERUKA, "THE RITUAL
OF SIGNS AND MUDRAS OF ALL THE YOGINIS" IS THE
TWENTIETH CHAPTER.

21. The Ritual of Viewing Characteristics of the Limbs of the Mudra

Next, the explanation of
The view of the great secret.

The woman who touches her crown,
To that one show your head.

Whoever shows her forehead,
To that one show your cheek.

Whoever shows her teeth,
To that one show your tongue.

Whoever shows her lips,
To that one show your chin.

Whoever shows her neck,
To that one show your stomach.

Whoever shows her hand,
To that one show your shoulder.

Whoever shows the triple waist,
To that one show your back.

Whoever shows her breast,
To that one show your chin.

Whoever shows her stomach,
To that one show your navel.

Whoever shows her secret [organ],
To that one show your penis.

Whoever shows her thigh,
To that one show your anus.

Whoever shows her knee,
To that one show the calf of your leg.

Whoever shows the sole of her foot,
To that one show the sole of your foot.

Whoever shows the joint of her finger,
To that one show your fingernail.

Whoever shows the earth,
To that one show the sky.

Whoever shows the sky,
To that one show the sun.

Whoever shows the river,
To that one show the ocean.

Have no doubt that these are the
Bodily mudras of the dakinis.
These secrets should always be displayed
By showing them perfectly as one proceeds.

FROM THE SPEECH OF GLORIOUS HERUKA, "THE RITUAL OF
VIEWING CHARACTERISTICS OF THE LIMBS OF THE MUDRA"
IS THE TWENTY-FIRST CHAPTER.

22. The Ritual of the Particular Characteristics of the Mudras

Now for further explanations of
The ritual of the limbs of the mudra
By which one will know without a doubt
Who are one's brothers and sisters.

By showing one finger
It is saying "welcome."

By showing two fingers
It is saying "welcome" in response.

This is the supreme explanation
Of the mudras of the limbs of all yoginis.

The middle left finger is extended
And the forefinger a little bent;
One should know this is the eye mudra.
When the mantrika shows her that,
As long as he lives
Have no doubt that she
Will come under his control.

Whoever shows the middle finger,
To that one show the forefinger.

Whoever shows the ring finger,
To that one show the tongue.

Whoever shows the trident [mudra],
To that one show the spear [mudra].

Whoever shows the crown of the head,
To that one show the hair part.

Whoever shows the ground,
To that one show the sky.

Whoever shows a wrathful expression,
To that one show the hair part.

Whoever shows the teeth,
To that one show the lips.

Whoever shows the neck,
To that one show the mouth.

Whoever shows the forehead,
To that one show the eyes.

This is the series of mudras
Of the limbs of all the dakinis.
These are always shown by the secret ones
Who proceed with pure view.

FROM THE SPEECH OF GLORIOUS HERUKA, "THE RITUAL OF
THE PARTICULAR CHARACTERISTICS OF THE MUDRAS" IS THE
TWENTY-SECOND CHAPTER.

23. The Ritual of the Characteristics of the Particular Sign Mudras of the Dakinis

Next, I will perfectly explain
The manifestations of the dakinis
Through which the hero can understand even from a distance
Who is the sister of the hero.

[She] who is the basis and the earth
Possesses the commitments and is passionate.
[She] is the basis of the enjoyment of the hero.
Taking her as the basis and support,
She should be offered and bound to the yogi.

These are the yoginis who
Look with [the] head turned backward,
[The] face transforming
As the eyebrows move to indicate bliss.

One should know immediately
The variety [of their appearances]
That have thus arisen from the dakinis.

Three completely round lines should be known through
Turning and transforming.
One should know all the characteristics
Of the dakinis who definitely go
And suddenly return.

Her face becomes frightening, as before,
Whose aspect is clearly like a vajra,
The sound of [her] voice like a cuckoo;
It is clear that she is supreme.[33]

She has these signs in her house:
[Something] like a vajra together with a mirror.
The second also transforms as well:
[Something] like a sword and a mirror,
Always like a spear and a victory banner.
The embrace should be known through a mirror.

The characteristics of these forms
Should be known briefly.
[Those] endowed with these characteristics
Should be known as supreme dakinis.[34]

FROM THE SPEECH OF GLORIOUS HERUKA, "THE RITUAL OF
THE CHARACTERISTICS OF THE PARTICULAR SIGN MUDRAS
OF THE DAKINIS" IS THE TWENTY-THIRD CHAPTER.

---

33. The sTog Palace edition says, "The suchness of that is clearly supreme."
34. These last four lines do not appear in the sTog Palace edition.

24. The Ritual of the Imputed Signs of the Symbolic Words of All the Characteristics of the Four Classes

And then a further symbolic language
Will here be explained to the practitioner.
Have no doubt you will become aware
Who is a brother or sister.

Po Tang Ki means "to speak honestly."
Pa Ti Po Tang Ki means "to reply honestly."
Ka Mu means "to go away."
Lum Pa means "to come."
Te Ham is what is said for a "city."
Tsa Tu Ka is said for "take!"
Bhri Ta Na means the "heart itself."
Koa Wa means "death."[35]
Ka Ra Ni Ka is "bell."
Ah Li is "head."
Ba Rha Ha is "hair."
Shra Wa Na is "ear."
Ah Mi Ta Sa Ta is "to churn."
Sa Ma Ka Ma is "people."
Ta Li Ka is "dakini."
Na Ra Kam is "mandala."
Ah Mu Kam is "charnel ground."

35. In the sTog Palace edition it says, "*Marana* means 'bad sound.'" What this variant reading indicates is just that the term and its gloss have been reversed in the sTog edition. Thus, *marana* is the Sanskrit word translated above as "death," whereas its gloss, "bad sound" (Tib. *sgra ngan*), is a translation of Skt. *kaurava*.

Ka Ki La is "door."

Shra Sa is "the lineage of a Brahman."

Pa Ri Dhi is "the lineage of a king."

Bir Ti is "the lineage of a master."

Tru Ta is "the lineage of commoners."

An Dya Sata is "butcher."

Ba Shu Li Ka is "housewife."

Bha Ki is "dakini."

Me Ka is "water."

Gri Ha Ne is "the sign of the mudra."

Che So La Rek Pa is saying "we are hungry."

Tri Sha Na Ni is "to infuse."[36]

Kan Dha Bha Si Ni is "thirst."

Ku Ta means "coming from such and such a place."

Kir Na is "flower."

Tu lam pa is "to laugh."

Da Ra is "tooth."

Ni Ro Dha is "to rain."

Tri Pa Ti is "to request."

Dhu Ra Yu is "outside."

Dhu Pa Tri Ya is "cloud."

Sah Nu is "mountain."

Sa Ri Ta is "river."

Ang Gu Li is "hands and limbs."

Pa Da na is "face."

Radza Ka is "tongue."

Ah Da Na is "tooth."

Bak Ti is "victory banner."

Tsan Do is "rosary."

Tsa la is "wind."

Tra Pha Ha is "boat."

Pa Shu is "deer."

Yan Ti is "mandala."

---

36. This line does not appear in the Phugdrag edition. It and the next line are the reverse of one another.

Na Ra Kam is "commitment."[37]
Sa Sa Ma is "intersection of four roads."
Phel Khu Sham is "living being."
Ma Ha Kram is "the great victim."
Kha is "born as a goat."
Na is said for "person."
Go is said for "bull."
Ma is said for "buffalo."
Bha is "eating."
Ha is its synonym.
Ah Bi Ka is "royal personage."
Touching the breast is "abiding in solitude."
Touching the mouth is "I have eaten."
Touching the teeth is saying "contentment."
Ho is sometimes its synonym.
Hri is "shame."
Touching the empty is "nonexistent."
Touching the thigh is "you have sexual intercourse (*maithuna*)."
From above is saying "do it that way."
Evam means "not from below."

These mudras, reply mudras, and secret signs are the characteristics of the four classes that were taught by the hero.

FROM THE SPEECH OF GLORIOUS HERUKA, "THE RITUAL OF THE IMPUTED SIGNS OF THE SYMBOLIC WORDS OF ALL THE CHARACTERISTICS OF THE FOUR CLASSES" IS THE TWENTY-FOURTH CHAPTER.

---

37. This line from the sTog Palace edition does not appear in the Phugdrag edition.

25. The Ritual of the Secret Root Mantra

Next, these eight were attached to
The end [of the root mantra] and hidden to
Fulfill all of the aims of one's desires because
Sentient beings are of little devotion and
Confused with a mind bereft of wisdom.

In that regard the hero and yoginis clearly taught this secret mantra:

OM NAMO BHAGAWATE WIRE SHAYA
MAHA KALPA AHGNI SAMNI BHAYA
DZATA MAGUTRA KRORTAYA
DAMKHATRA KARA LOTRA BHIKANA MUKAYA
SAHARA BHUDZA BHASU RAYA
PARASHUPA SHODYADA SHULA KATVANGA DHARINE
BHEGADZINAM BARA DHARAYA
MAHA DHUMBA ANDHAKARA WABUKAYA[38]

KARA KARA, KURU KURU, BENDHA BENDHA, TRASAYA TRA-
SAYA, KYOMBHAYA KYOMBHAYA, HROM HROM, HRAH HRAH,
PHEIM PHEIM, PHAT PHAT, DAHA DAHA, PATSA PATSA, BHAKYA
BHAKYA, BASA RUDHI, RATNA MALA WALAMBINI, GRIHANA
GRIHANA, SAPTA PATALA GATA, BHUDZAGAM SARWABA, TAR-
DZAYA TARDZAYA, AKANDYA AKANDYA, HRIM HRIM, GYON

---

38. By adding OM at the beginning and HUM HUM PHAT at the end of these eight lines, they become the eight lines of praise to Heruka. What follows is the root mantra itself.

GYON, KYAMA KYAMA, HAM HAM, HIM HIM, HUM HUM, KILI
KILI, SILI SILI, HILI HILI, DHILI DHILI, HUM HUM PHAT[39]

FROM THE SPEECH OF GLORIOUS HERUKA, "THE RITUAL
OF THE SECRET ROOT MANTRA" IS THE TWENTY-FIFTH
CHAPTER.

---

39. For an explanation of this and all other mantras in this text, see Trijang Rinpoche's commentary on the *Chakrasamvara Root Tantra* in volume 2 of *Source of Supreme Bliss*, trans. David Gonsalez (Seattle: Dechen Ling Press, 2010).

26. The Ritual of Thoroughly Investigating the Disciple, and the Vows

Furthermore, through the knowledge of
The mantra of glorious Heruka,
Which does not exist in the three worlds,
Completely forsake all [other] secret mantras.

The messengers abide perfectly
In forward and reverse order,
Bestowing attainments above and below.
My messengers go everywhere;
The messengers bestow all attainments.

Seeing and likewise touching,
Kissing and always embracing,
Especially the place of the yoga,
As long as there are collections of yogi[nis]
It is said they will accomplish all attainments.

The actual entities should all be given
And never to others.
The messengers may abide as
Mothers, sisters, daughters, and wives.
Always offering the mantra.
This is explained as the ritual of suchness.

And now I will explain the commitments
In the yoga tantras, so difficult to find.

Going to the left of one born as a woman
Bestows the desired attainments.

Those staying in [her] house or field
Should be known even if far away.
The yoga of Shri Heruka is supreme.
The master is the yogini herself.
The practitioner of this tantra
Is perfectly established indeed.

Do not despise and do not abandon.
You should make [as many] offerings as you are able
To Crowface (Kakasya) and to the other eight, and by so doing
Your faith and respect will increase and
They will become the cause of everlasting attainments.

Protect all [your] commitments.
Do not desire union with
Another goddess out of ignorance.
Be nondual, and be unobstructed.[40]
Perform the conduct of the commitments.
Perfectly embrace a powerful woman.
Have Brahma conduct[41] in one's mental stabilization.
Avoid being angry with the flow of fluids.
These eight commitments should all be practiced.[42]

Abiding in the sadhana
The practitioner should know them all.
They are common to all tantras and
Cannot be destroyed without a cause.
They should be accepted through faith itself,

40. This line is different in the Phugdrag and sTog Palace editions.
41. That is, chastity (Tib. *tshangs spyod*; Skt. *brahmacarya*).
42. These are the eight uncommon commitments of mother tantra. For a listing of and commentary on these eight, see Sermey Khensur Lobsang Tharchin, *Six- Session Guru Yoga* (Howell, NJ: Mahayana Sutra and Tantra Press, 1999).

Not by the eyes or by the hand.
Do not reveal this secret,
And make great effort to keep it hidden.

The wise should move the little finger where
The messengers perfectly reside.
Concerning the practitioners, there are three:
The pure, the impure, and the mixed.
There are the impartial, the pure, and
The person illuminated with good qualities.

FROM THE SPEECH OF GLORIOUS HERUKA, "THE RITUAL OF
THOROUGHLY INVESTIGATING THE DISCIPLE, AND THE VOWS"
IS THE TWENTY-SIXTH CHAPTER.

27. The Rituals of Activity, Conduct, Offering, and the Tormas

Next, the conduct of the hero
Who perfectly accomplishes all the dakinis.

By understanding the divisions of the characteristics
You will quickly produce the attainments.
Going from this city to that city,
The physical attributes of the messenger are
Similar to a sword blade
That increases and purifies merit.
So, by associating with the messengers
The practitioner will attain realizations.

They are accomplished quickly
Even without offerings, recitation, or concentration
By the practitioner with mantra and mudra.
The offering itself is an excellent engagement.
As there are no offerings other than this,
This is the definitive teaching
Of the joyous path of the messengers.

The practitioner who strives for the attainments,
Perfectly endowed with knowledge mantras and mudras,
Should always eat the *tsaru* offerings.
With excellent meditative equipoise the practitioner
Should practice with all lineages.
Do not eat without examining.

With the inseparable suchness
There are two ways of accomplishing the messengers.
When performing the ritual of attainments
The messengers are only one.
As one delights in the attainments,
The attainments are summoned and
Are perfectly endowed with mantra.
By receiving empowerment from the lineage of gurus
And by speaking perfectly to the messengers,
[Become] accustomed to union with the mudra
Produced from the cause of complete exalted wisdom.

The nature of mind arises at dawn
By moving the whole body with
The weapons that transcend the limbs.
Continuously reciting the mantra,
Enjoy all the places of the body
Through the actions that purify the body.

Definitely revealing the places of yoga,
You should not step over the weapons.
[The one] endowed with commitments does not become angry.
Do not transcend effort.
Together engage in joy.
With the aim of liberation and the aim of bliss,
Engage in the actions of the commitments.

The mind is liberated by wandering,[43]
Always naked at night and
Always black and red.

Necklaces, bangles, head ornaments,
Earrings, brahmin's thread, and
A rosary of human heads as a necklace,

---

43. The sTog Palace edition says, "One is not released from mental creations."

A sash of small bells creating sounds,
Hair tied in a topknot and bound by silk,
Adorned with artificial hair and so forth,
A khatvanga staff possessing a vajra skull,
Beating a *damaru* drum and making the sound HUM,
All the heroes and heroines
Are adorned with the three types of armor and
Wear the limbs of sentient beings as earrings.[44]

[Those who] desire bliss should produce bliss,
Completely abandon the breast ornament,[45]
And dwell in the purity of Shri Heruka.
The practitioner who desires the attainments
Should be perfectly endowed with the five mudras,
With necklaces, bangles, and
Jeweled ornaments for the crown of the head.

Always abide in the aspect with
Breast ornament and ash,
Always displayed at night
And secretly during the day,
Hide well the exalted wisdom actions,
Be perfectly pacified and without fatigue.
Purity should be known as threefold,
And it abides within one's own continuum.

Do not view them according to class;
Abandon binding [one's hair] on the crown of your head and so forth.
The first purity is the messenger,
The second is acknowledged as *soma*,
And eating tsaru food
Is explained to be the third purity.

---

44. The paragraph above is found only in the Phugdrag edition, not the sTog Palace edition.
45. Tib. *mchod phyir thogs*; Skt. *yajñopavīta*. This term refers to the breast ornament worn by brahmins when making offerings.

Protecting the purities, the
Yogi is always pure.
Gradually attaining the state of complete purity,
How will attainments not arise?

That which is taught in the *Essence of Suchness* (*Tattvasamgraha*)
Is also taught in the *Samvara*
And perfectly explained in the *Secret Tantra*.
This was taught as well in the *First Supreme Glory* (*Paramadya*)
And in the *Vajrabhairava Tantra*.[46]
It bestows the attainments of recitation, conduct, and so forth.
By mere concentration on that,
In one instant the mantrika becomes realized.
The joys on the path of yoga
Are explained as pure conduct.

It is not possible to explain
The merits of purity that occur and
The extensive good qualities of the practitioner.

How would one be able to express
With one mouth only
What cannot be explained
Even with a hundred thousand mouths?

All the characteristics of purity are
The great exalted wisdom of glorious Heruka.
The blisswater of the practitioner is
Not two and nondual,
Touched by the union of nonduality;
The holy river destroys negativities.
By touching and also by speaking
One is liberated from all negativities.

46. For bibliographical references to these scriptures and speculation regarding the ambiguous *Samvara* (Tib. *bde mchog*) and *Secret Tantra* (Tib. *gsang ba'i rgyud*; Skt. *guhyatantra*), see Gray 2007, 279.

The pure body is free of faults.
Through every great being's engaging in the conduct
All negativities are purified and
The state of a tathagata is attained.
All negativities are purified,
One is born into the lineage of the tathagata and
Becomes a king endowed with faith.

Thus always make offerings and
Respectfully offer tormas
That the yogi should give according to the ritual
For the desired actions on the tenth days of the
Waning moon and the waxing moon.
With great effort make offerings
With intoxicants and meat to the vajra goddesses.

The respectful person who has
Become delighted in Heruka makes offerings.
For that purpose the supreme state is in [your] hands.
Contented, they bestow the supreme [attainments],
Engage in night conduct and offer tormas.
Naked, let your hair down
As Shri Heruka.
Just so, the mothers become delighted by embrace.

FROM THE SPEECH OF GLORIOUS HERUKA, "THE RITUALS OF ACTIVITY, CONDUCT, OFFERING, AND THE TORMAS" IS THE TWENTY-SEVENTH CHAPTER.

28. The Ritual of Inner Fire Offering and Being Endowed with One Lineage

Perfect offerings pure in nature
Made to the hero who has arisen from nirvana
And offerings [made] to oneself
[Become] offerings to all the collection of buddhas.

All the heroes and yoginis
Moving and at rest,
With the peaceful collection make offerings to[47]
The brothers as well as the heroes who perfectly abide.

Together the brothers and the sons
Are the source of happiness and suffering.
Do not disclose to them the mantras,
Mudras, or exalted wisdom.

Oneself should use the tsaru food
And always engage in the practice of the commitments.
Do not give secret mantra to anyone
Nor allow the oral instructions to degenerate.[48]

---

47. This expression, "peaceful collection" (Tib. *zhi ba'i 'dus*), refers to a collection of *soma*, which Indian commentators, as Gray notes (2007, 283), interpreted as meaning both "liquor" and "semen." In Trijang Rinpoche's commentary on the body mandala of Ghantapa in *The Ecstatic Dance of Chakrasamvara*, trans. David Gonsalez (Seattle: Dechen Ling Press, 2013), he equates the "peaceful drink" with the inner offering.
48. The sTog Palace edition says, "Do not bestow the oral instructions."

It should only be given to those
Who abide in the commitments.

Do not abandon the messengers for others
And wander out of ignorance and attachment.
The messengers always desire liberation
And transcend enjoyments.

Do not stay with those of lower birth
And don't act with disrespect.
Mothers, sisters, and daughters and
Wives are the very abode of the messengers.

Asceticism is definitely rejected.
Such are the attainments of the mandala.
The mandala is accomplished in such a way
That one draws forth the supreme.
The substances are thus ascertained.

In the world always practice from the left.
Always proceed with the left leg.
Change [to] the left hand.
The left side conduct is the best offering.

By merely embracing from the left
And offering food with the left,
Your conduct will not degenerate but will
Become complete.

The practitioner persevering in the actions,
Performing the commitments of the lineage, and
Practicing eating together,[49]
Are all the practices of the five lineages,

49. Tib. *gcig du zas.*

And are recognized as the four lineages as well.
In one lineage are all the practices.

The perfect offering to [the one] accomplished in yoga
Is cow meat, horse meat, dog meat, and a variety of others,
Performed in a triangle mandala;
Even the buddhas will be definitely destroyed.

Endowed with perfect mudra and mantra,
It is thus the food of the heroes,
The emanation of Shri Heruka.

Abandon the actions of all treatises.
The mind of the exalted wisdom of nondual yoga[50]
Should always be apprehended.
The protection of all actions
Is accomplished without obstruction;
There is no other means of accomplishment.

The good and excellent messenger
Is caring and endowed with effort.
Thoroughly desiring perfect union
She induces the substance of yoga.
Delighting in the oral instructions of the guru,
Her purpose is to be comparable to the *Giver of Wealth*.

From the speech of glorious Heruka, "The Ritual of Inner Fire Offering and Being Endowed with One Lineage" is the twenty-eighth chapter.

---

50. This line is not in the Phugdrag edition.

29. The Ritual of the Characteristics of the Messengers and the Means of Abiding in Power

Next are further teachings:
One should know the characteristics of the messengers
By which one comes to a perfect understanding
Of the dakinis who abide in the commitments.

Seeing in an instant the brother and father
And even the Lord himself,
She has a thick tongue and orange eyes and
Rough hair that is orange as well.

One with all the common attainments and
Always delighting in recitation and conducts
And endowed with perfect mindfulness,
She is connected to the state of the messengers.
The twenty-four supreme dakinis
Bestow the best fruit of enjoyment and liberation.

Always recite the root mantra.
It is the means to accomplish all of your desires.
It pacifies all the demons.
The moving and unmoving in the three worlds—
A treasure of the fruit of the play of yoga—
Arises from this secret mantra.

Perfectly endowed with mantra and mudra,
The practitioner makes effort in the attainments.

With secret mantra devoid of the mudra
One will not attain the three bodies.
Until the practices of heat,
Make effort in conceptual [yoga].[51]

Whoever is hostile toward this great yoga
Which accomplishes all of the desired aims
Will be reborn as a dog a hundred times
And then be born as a butcher.

For example, by desiring some butter and
Making effort at churning water,
Not only will you not get butter
But you will only exhaust yourself.

To rely on other yogas
By offering and withholding
As a means of livelihood
Is [completely] meaningless.

Whatever place is inhabited
By a yogi or supreme hero,
Even if low caste or barbarian,
That region is a favored one.
In order to care for living beings
I shall always abide there.

FROM THE SPEECH OF GLORIOUS HERUKA, "THE RITUAL OF
THE CHARACTERISTICS OF THE MESSENGERS AND THE MEANS
OF ABIDING IN POWER" IS THE TWENTY-NINTH CHAPTER.

---

51. I interpret "heat" (Tib. *dro ba*; Skt. *ushma*) as *tummo*, which is part of the completion stage for
which a synonym is "nonconceptual yoga." The phrase "make effort in the conceptual" seems to
be referring to the generation stage, for which a synonym is "conceptual yoga." However, the
term "heat" may well imply the third of the four stages of the path of preparation. At this point
in the generation stage, you would transfer to the noncontrived completion stage.

30. The Ritual of Mantra Selection Bound in the Muraja Drum

And then further explanation:
It is very difficult to find the chart.
For the one with mere knowledge [of this]
Quickly attains realization.

In a place where the ground is level and pleasing and
Anointed with sandalwood,
Saffron water and perfume,
Spread flower arrangements and
A rosary of perfectly arranged butter lamps.
Delight with the scent of incense,
Do all of this yourself;
Bind them and so forth in all directions.

Next bind with the *muraja* drum[52]
The nine lines and the circle,
Draw equally the last letter
Arranged perfectly with concentration.

From that place select the hero
[Who accomplishes] all of your desired aims.
[Extracting them] in serial and reverse order,
The practitioner takes that number
Of vowels and consonants

52. Thanks to David Gray for the Sanskrit name of this drum (Tib. *rdza rnga*).

And arranges them inside; they are
Accomplished by the practitioner of virtue.

From that calculation,
Take the thirty-second chart,
Distinguished by the fifth.
Take half of one hundred,
Distinguished by the twenty-fourth.
Extract the thirty-sixth chart,
Distinguished particularly by the third.
Take the thirty-second,
Distinguished by the fifth.
Then hold the twenty-fifth,
Attaching the twenty-fourth.
Correctly extract the thirty-third,
Possessing the fifteenth chart, and join them
Perfectly together with the fifth.
[This is] the first line, said to be
Supremely beautiful.

Extracting the nineteenth chart,
Perfectly endowed with the son of fire, it is
Distinguished by the diagram of the third.
The eighth seed of the semivowels
Is endowed with the thirty-sixth chart;
Thus you will correctly possess the syllables.
Again these lines themselves are
The means of accomplishing all your wishes.
And then by extracting the self-arisen,
Attach it to the fifth chart,
Conjoined at the top with a *nada* and drop.
The second line is explained to be
The means of accomplishing all one's desired aims.

The nineteenth chart itself is
Distinguished by the twenty-seventh,
And correctly possesses the third.

Adopting correctly the thirty-third,
Attach the second chart
That correctly possesses the twentieth.
This is the beautiful and supreme.
The twenty-first itself is
Likewise endowed with the twenty-sixth.
Reciting the words twice,
Enter into meditative concentration,
Then reverse the order and
Take the first from the chart,
Perfectly endowed with the end of the fourth and
Likewise together with the fifteenth.
The third line is explained to be
Desiring the meaning of Dharma and liberation.

Take the seed which is the second chart,
The thirty-sixth from the chart,
And likewise the twenty-sixth and
Perfectly extract the thirty-third,
Endowed with the thirteenth chart.
From that chart extract the tenth,
The practitioner having reversed the order.

From the chart, select the nineteenth,
Likewise the twenty-ninth chart,
Perfectly endowed with the second diagram,
Adorned with a nada and a drop.[53]
Then, take the seed of water,[54]
Distinguished by the son of fire
With the eighth as well.

By attaching the syllable HUM at the end,
This is called the "King of the Three Realms,"
Adorned by the four mantra letters,

---

53. The Phugdrag edition reads "sound" (Tib. *sgra*), which is another name for the nada diacritic.
54. The sTog Palace edition says "take the lord of the earth."

OM[55] which illuminates all, and with
HUM and PHAT attached to the end.

The mantra of the *Wheel Turning King of Knowledge*
Has not arisen and will not arise
In the *Tattvasamgraha*, *Paramadya*,
Samvara, or *Vajrabhairava*.

Perfectly endowed with four wrathful [faces],
And instantly transforming into eight bodies,
For the sake of protecting the wheel of bliss,
Particularly from all the vicious ones,
By merely discovering this and
Without needing to analyze it, they will die.
Recite it in union with the mandala
And the fruits of all the attainments will arise.

OM SUMBHA NISUMBHA HUM HUM PHAT
OM GRIHANA GRIHANA HUM HUM PHAT
OM GRIHANA PAYA GRIHANA PAYA HUM HUM PHAT
OM ANAYA HO BAGHAWAN VIDYA RADZA VAJRA HUM HUM
    PHAT

FROM THE SPEECH OF GLORIOUS HERUKA, "THE RITUAL OF
MANTRA SELECTION BOUND IN THE MURAJA DRUM" IS THE
THIRTIETH CHAPTER.

---

55. The sTog Palace edition says OM and the Phugdrag edition says AH.

31. The Ritual of the Hand Signals of Food, the Fire Offering, and Tormas

And then all the great meats
Are explained to be generated as the *Vajra Terrifier*.
This is explained to be the *Horrible Terrifier*
Of all wicked ones.

Engage in eating, burned offerings, and tormas
With dog and pig flesh as well as
Fowl, and without distinction.
Accomplish everything without exception
And all kingdoms will be perfectly accomplished.

Who can criticize the skullcup [relic] of someone
Endowed with the body of the dharmakaya
Arising as the three symbols of
Conch shells, pearls, and oyster shells?

The hero possesses a rosary of skulls and is
Adorned by the aspect of a half-moon.
Appearing in that way
He is said to be the hero of all heroes.

The practitioner should display the five signs
With the left hand.
The [left hand] is where the Hero resides,
Engaging in the signs.

The three realms, moving and unmoving, and
All beings arise from the left.

Vajrasattva abides in the thick one,[56]
The thin one[57] is also Vairochana,
The principal[58] is at Pema Kardze.
This is the best way of bestowing and
Stabilizing all the attainments of the hero.

Akashagarbha is at the little finger
Endowed with an inexhaustible body.
The surface of the fingernail is
Said to transform into the abode of Hayagriva.

All of these arise
From the hero's left.

In the palm of the hand is Heruka
Joyously united with Vajravarahi.
Behind that from the very definite
You should display the fifth sign.

These are arranged in the hand
And where all food is collected.[59]
Through such a ritual
One should make offerings to the sacred hero.

The earth is said to be Lochana,
The water element is called Mamaki,
Fire is called Pandara,

56. The thumb.
57. The index finger.
58. The ring finger.
59. The Phugdrag edition has "lovers" (Tib. *mdza' ba*), whereas the sTog Palace edition has "food" (Tib. *bza' ba*). Since this section is an explanation of the "hand offering," which is a method for eating one's food as nectar, I have chosen "food" over "lovers."

Air is called Tara,
Chumbika is emptiness
As well as the perfections.
In the center all the heroes abide,
Brought behind [the hand] by the skilled.

Do not speak of this secret and
Make a strong effort to keep it hidden.
In that way the signs of the heroes
Should be undertaken together with tsaru food.
All the heroes are united,
Heruka is the web of the dakinis.

FROM THE SPEECH OF GLORIOUS HERUKA, "THE RITUAL OF THE HAND SIGNALS OF FOOD, THE FIRE OFFERING, AND TORMAS" IS THE THIRTY-FIRST CHAPTER.

32. The Ritual of Accomplishing Animals, Sacrificial Animals, Zombies, and the Generation Stage

Next, the further explanation of
The assembly of food and tormas
Through which, if the correct ritual is done,
One will quickly achieve the attainments.

These procedures of summoning sacrificial animals[60]
Were previously explained.
The sacrificial animals are therefore five:
Donkeys, turtles, people, camels,
Jackals, horses, and so forth.
Attainments are accomplished in the mandala of
These animals that are the branches of realization.

From among the lineages is "the supreme sacrificial animal."
From the four-limbed, the elephant;
From birds, the goose itself;
From the animals, the turtle;
And from the gods, the moving lips.[61]
They are explained in this way
To be the sacrificial animals
In the mandala of accomplishing attainments.

60. In Tibetan *phyugs* literally means "animal" or "beast," but here, since the animals and their flesh are used for ritual, I added "sacrificial."
61. On this term, see Gray 2007, 301n5.

A raven, waterfowl, jackal,
The twice-born one[62] and a great aristocrat,[63]
A laughing crane, a *kadamba* goose.
By making food [offerings], fire offerings, and torma [offerings],
All of one's desires are accomplished.

With the milk of a black female dog,[64]
Together with black lentils and rice,
Follow your desires, be fearless and
Perform the fire offering in the mouth of a corpse
Up to one hundred and eight times.

Then the ghost will rise up, asking
The practitioner questions and saying
"Whatever you say I will do."

Going underground, the sword,
As well as annihilating or benefiting,
Treasure, eye ointment, or pill,
The swift footed, and taking the essence;
One of these entities will be bestowed,
It will not go elsewhere.
Accomplishing the messengers above and below,
Have no doubts about this tantra.

Floating above the place of cows,
Leftover dry grass,
Likewise make a great conch shell,
Its nature is great bliss,
Or a perfect tortoise.
These will bestow realization.

62. According to Gray (2007, 301n6; following Sachen Kunga Nyingpo), this is a parrot.
63. Gray (2007, 301n7; again reading Sachen) says this is an owl.
64. The sTog Palace edition only says "black dog" and does not include the feminine particle *mo*.

[Heruka] has four hands and four faces,
Up to a hundred thousand hands,
With an extremely wrathful white body
And maintaining a fearful form,
Looking at Vajravarahi,
Her body is his color and she is holding weapons.

The hero has a rosary of skulls,
His body is smeared with ash,
His hair is in a tiara, and he has a spear,
His body is adorned by mudras
And his face is showing the fangs a little,
And the great hungry ghost is used as a seat.

At all times the practitioner,
Meditating with the knowledge of mantra,
Will attain the desired realizations,
All the special superior qualities.

FROM THE SPEECH OF GLORIOUS HERUKA, "THE RITUAL OF
ACCOMPLISHING ANIMALS, SACRIFICIAL ANIMALS, ZOMBIES,
AND THE GENERATION STAGE" IS THE THIRTY-SECOND
CHAPTER.

33. The Ritual of the Secret Offering and Offering Respect

Next, not all the supreme practitioners
Are [realized] in all yogas
And are able to consume to the extent of their abilities,
Food, drink, fish, meat, and so forth.
Even if you don't have these you should regard them
As the five [nectars][65] and eat them.

Extensively partake of food and drink
And always perform at night,
After which the messenger should be bestowed.

In particular the practitioner should
Place his head in her lap and make perfect
Offerings to her as the nondual hero.
Embrace with mothers as well as sisters or
Daughters or one's wife.
Undertaking this according to the ritual,
One will be liberated from bondage.

After that, one will accomplish the mantra
As long as it arises.
Abiding perfectly in the body of the master,
I, the hero, will accept the offerings
From the practitioner.

65. The addition of the word "nectar" is according to David Gray's interpretation.

Have no doubts that the abode of
The heroes are the mudras themselves.

The practitioner with good concentration
Should sing, dance, and so forth.
As long as all living beings do not
Cherish the wisdom of yoga,
Living beings will continue to circle in samsara and
Suffering and misery will continue to flow.

The practitioner should offer
All of his belongings to the mudra.
By offering that which one covets,
Or [doing so] with contempt, one will definitely be burned.

The persons of yoga tantra should
Make offerings with perfect effort.
The yogi offers all things to
The primordially accomplished Mahamudra.
Later the heroes should
Practice heroism itself.

Thus having made offerings,
The practitioner [will be able]
To go underground and
Resurrect [the dead].
He [will attain] peace and increase,
Power and summoning,
Killing, separating, and so forth.
Making beings dull and rigid
And other such things such as
Dividing and annihilating.

Having offered the attainment of actions,
Whatever actions are appropriate
Will be accomplished without trouble.

Have no doubt that the practitioner
Will attain all these realizations.

FROM THE SPEECH OF GLORIOUS HERUKA, "THE RITUAL OF THE SECRET OFFERING AND OFFERING RESPECT" IS THE THIRTY-THIRD CHAPTER.

34. The Ritual of the Actions of the Burned Offering of the Nondual Messenger

Next, the extensive ritual called
The "wheel of the net of the dakinis."
Have no doubt that whatever actions are
Undertaken by the practitioner are quickly [accomplished].

All the heroes and yoginis
Must abide in the centers of the lotuses,
Entering between the eyebrows
And thus abiding in the central channel.

[Offer] food and burned offerings
To the parched mouth of the hero
Earnestly with the five burned offerings
Of meat and blood.

And then ignite the fire,
Offer the nine fire sacrifices,
And place them in a blazing ocean.

The wheel should face all directions,
Likewise the four faces of the powerful hero and
The abode of the hero.
On the petals are four female messengers,
The nondual bliss of all heroes.

Through such a ritual
Bestow Khandaroha outside,

Abiding in their own forms
And viewed as being in the centers of the mandalas,
Clarified in these mandalas.
You should follow these stages correctly.

Thus in the *Ocean of Knowledge*
[This was] briefly taught by the hero.
Oneself is unified with the nondual messengers.
Have no doubt you will accomplish this.

FROM THE SPEECH OF GLORIOUS HERUKA, "THE RITUAL OF
THE ACTIONS OF THE BURNED OFFERING OF THE NONDUAL
MESSENGER" IS THE THIRTY-FOURTH CHAPTER.

35. The Ritual of the Actions of Nonduality and Cheating Untimely Death

Next, the supreme and excellent actions
That symbolize the appropriate stages,
The offerings with the nature of the nondual union,
Applied to the individual actions are
The perfect accomplishing actions of the mantra.
Their divisions will be explained sequentially.

The mantra of the messengers, their colors, and so forth
Turn with the force of an arrow,
Back and forth by the bow of secret mantra.
The distinction is made according to their placement,
Holding a rosary of seeds with
HUM attached at the end.

Snatching the object of accomplishment,
He will never go further than one step.
Facing each other in union,
Bind them with the vajra chain.
Separate them with the vajra,
Likewise turn them like a bee.

Summon them with a hook,
Churn them in the manner of a pestle.
It is said they are struck by a vajra.

Attaching the arrow to the breath[66]
[You will be] victorious in cheating untimely death.
Attaching the khatvanga staff to the limbs,
The skullcup offering vessel
Is the weapon definitely attached to the face.

FROM THE SPEECH OF GLORIOUS HERUKA, "THE RITUAL OF
THE ACTIONS OF NONDUALITY AND CHEATING UNTIMELY
DEATH" IS THE THIRTY-FIFTH CHAPTER.

66. While the sTog Palace edition says "breath" (Tib. *dbugs*), the Phugdrag edition says "hole" (Tib. *phug*).

36. The Offering of Suchness and the Ritual of Action

And then the great offering of the mudra,
Famed as the arrangement of the mantra,[67]
Quickly performing the attainments,
Have no doubt about this offering of the mudra.

Attach the mantra to the two signs [male and female],
The hero and dakini are nondual.
The essence [mantra] should be done likewise
And thus conjoin the dakini with the mantrika.

Churning the devout dakini,
The ritual of eating subdues the mudra.
With the power of the action and weapon and
Likewise with the essence [mantra]
One should likewise unite with the dakini.[68]
Her pure body is one's own desire.

By making offerings to the hero
You should make effort in this action.
The mantrika investigates with delight
And should definitely employ the reversal.

---

67. The Phugdrag edition says "the supreme glory" instead of "famed."
68. These verses refer to blessing the four places of the practitioner with the essence and close essence mantras of the father and mother.

For the purpose of annihilating and benefiting,
Meditate on the entity of actions.
By making the classifications of suchness,
Unify the path of the channels and
Perfectly accomplish the meaning of union.
Just as it is outside, it should be inside as well.
By this you will quickly accomplish
Gods and demigods, together with humans.

FROM THE SPEECH OF GLORIOUS HERUKA, "THE OFFERING OF SUCHNESS AND THE RITUAL OF ACTION" IS THE THIRTY-SIXTH CHAPTER.

37. The Ritual of Oneself Attaining Inner Power

And then a further explanation of
The ritual of overpowering [others'] bodies.
The mutual embrace of the secret mantra
Is applied to the dakinis in the same way.

Whatever food you eat
Should be vomited at the end of recitation and
Completed in seven nights;
Apply this to food and drink.
Through this, for as long as one lives
Have no doubt you will [bring others] under your control.

Drink light yellow butter and
Vomit it at the end of recitation.
If you then apply this to your face,
If you become angry with someone,
By merely looking at them you will gain control.

Crushing sesame oil and wild rice and
Anointing the body with them,
If the mantrika then carries this oil
This is the excellent way to prepare your food.
If you don't abandon this action,
For as long as you live you will always have control.

Through [those beings] eating
These pure black sesame seeds
Anointed with black mustard seeds,
Together the medicinal root *ruta*,[69] expelled from the anus,
And an intestinal worm born from karma,[70]
Prepared with one's own blood and semen,[71]
And applying the ointment perfectly [to their]
Food, drink, eye medicine, or clothing,
For as long as you live
Undoubtedly [they] will come under [your] power.

Burning bull meat in the burned offering
And anointing the deity with that blood,
In that moment [the deity] comes under one's power.
If it does not come it will die.

Place the [meat] in front of that very being
And through meditation skillfully perform the burned offering.
At the end of the burned offering offer the tormas.
In an instant the three worlds are summoned;
In seven nights the attainments will be accomplished.

In the three worlds it is difficult to find
The characteristic of one who practices the commitments.
By always keeping one's mantra hidden,
Making excellent effort and keeping it secret,
Not finding the hidden meaning
Those of lesser fortune will not accomplish it.

---

69. Tib. *ru rta*, translating Skt. *kushtha*, commonly known as *costus*.
70. The Phugdrag edition says "handborn" (Tib. *lag skyes*) where the sTog Palace edition reads "karma-born" (*las skyes*).
71. This translation follows the sTog Palace edition (Tib. *rang gi khrag dang btags nas ni / rang gi khu ba nyid dang sbyar*); cf. Gray 2007, 321. The Phugdrag edition gives a different reading of the second line (Tib. *rang gi khrag dang btags nas ni / sa shugs kra ni nyid dag dang*), thus reflecting *shukra,* the Sanskrit equivalent to Tib. *khu ba.*

Even the practitioner of little merit
Will discover it by pleasing [me].[72]

FROM THE SPEECH OF GLORIOUS HERUKA, "THE RITUAL OF
ONESELF ATTAINING INNER POWER" IS THE THIRTY-SEVENTH
CHAPTER.

72. This refers to pleasing the deity Heruka.

38. The Ritual of the Abode of the Secret Hero and the Place of Accomplishing the Yogini

Next are the signs and the dakinis,
What the characteristics of their bodies are, and
The distinctions of the limbs of the hero
By which the attainments are accomplished.

Do not draw the powerful hero.
Keep every aspect hidden and
Do not recite it in front of anyone.

The practitioner engages in all actions with the left,
Which is the secret characteristic of the dakini;
If [he then] indiscreetly recites the mantra
I will not look upon him.

This evil-natured one will be eaten
By many thousands of dakinis.
The one who destroys the commitments
And engages in bad actions,
And who without a doubt is killing brahmins,
This confused and wicked being,
This evil one, will become ransom
And will be eaten by the dakinis.
I will not protect you from that.

Among the secret beings,
The practitioner who damages the guru's commitments

Is like a sacrificial animal
And has fallen from the world of the Buddha.

The one who protects the
Tantra of glorious Heruka, so meaningful to behold,
Will be cherished and cared for by the dakinis.
I will benefit the practitioner who
Acts respectfully and sincerely
Toward the guru.

The dakinis will always be delighted;
Such is the source of all realizations.
This practitioner himself becomes a hero;
He will fly throughout the three realms, and
All the desires of the hero, the practitioner,
Will transform into offerings.

Engaging in that yoga
Offered purely, you will develop knowledge
By maintaining the conduct of Heruka.

If the practitioner of this tantra
Sees the master as the hero,
Seeing and seeing with every joy,
By proclaiming this supreme root secret mantra
Of the hero seven times,
The excellent mantra with HUM and so forth,
Then undertaking that practice with perseverance
Offered to all the buddhas and so forth,
And always to the great hero,
Have no doubt that [the hero] will be playful.

Vajravarahi abides in their heart together with
Myself, the hero, the yogini,
And the messengers.

They will see the merit of those beings and
The living beings of excellent birth.

Rivers, oceans, and ponds,
Mountains, crossroads,
A pool, a spring, and a small lake,
A thousand cities, and narrow streets:
In all of these places the yogini
Abides, looking at them all with passion.

Simultaneously the great hero
Plays with bliss
In a terrifying body of great strength
In the charnel grounds of great fear,
Enjoying the sky, and likewise underground,
With zombies and in smoke.

In a valley and a secret forest,
In all of these places
The yogini and secret people
Play with the practitioner.

FROM THE SPEECH OF GLORIOUS HERUKA, "THE RITUAL
OF THE ABODE OF THE SECRET HERO AND THE PLACE
OF ACCOMPLISHING THE YOGINI" IS THE THIRTY-EIGHTH
CHAPTER.

39. The Ritual of the View and HA HA Laughter

Next, the practitioner of this great yoga
Laughs with the eight aspects of mantra.
Through the pure vision [it]
Will undeniably be bestowed.

If the hero becomes terribly
Frightened and escapes [he will]
Hear many frightening sounds
From the unbearable, terrifying dakinis.

If the hero is not frightened,
Held by the left hand [he will]
Be carried by the dakinis to
Their own places,
Constantly frolicking
And led to the Blissful Abode.

With respect and desire for glorious Heruka
One is led to the astral state.
The practitioner endowed with the mantra body
Will neither die nor grow old in samsara.

FROM THE SPEECH OF GLORIOUS HERUKA, "THE RITUAL OF THE VIEW AND HA HA LAUGHTER" IS THE THIRTY-NINTH CHAPTER.

40. The Powerful Actions of the Five Lineages and Teachings on Mahamudra

This is the best explanation
By which earthlings can be subjugated.
Reciting the mantra of the hero, it is
Accomplished in one month by abiding in the ritual of yoga.

[For this purpose offer] intoxicants and lamps,
Together with fish and meat
To the powerful hero in all states.
The practitioner who performs the burned offering
For seven days at night with hand and mouth
Will receive extensive attainments.

By performing one hundred and eight [burned offerings],
If accomplished during the three times of the day,
The king together with his army
Will be subjugated in seven days.
By half [as many offerings], a great hero, and
By half of that, a person of high status.
A petty king [requires] thirty-two [burned offerings],
One should thus perform the burned offering in stages.

By offering the burned offering twenty times
Over seven days [one will subjugate] a brahmin.
Likewise seven [offerings are required] for the ruling class (*kshatriya*),
Five burned offerings for the noble class (*vaishya*), and
Three burned offerings for the common class (*shudra*).

One burned offering [is required] for the lowest of beings.
Thus if the hero performs this perfectly in stages
For one month,
By accomplishing the mantra of power
All migrators will be summoned.

The hero, through the previous ritual,
Will accomplish all of his wishes,
Or [he] will become the *Lord of Desire* on earth,
Or [he] will become glorious and fortunate.
Undoubtedly the practitioner
Will charm the dakinis.

FROM THE SPEECH OF GLORIOUS HERUKA, "THE POWERFUL
ACTIONS OF THE FIVE LINEAGES AND TEACHINGS ON
MAHAMUDRA" IS THE FORTIETH CHAPTER.

41. The Ritual of the Arrangement of the Twenty-Four Mandalas

Next, the supreme actions
By which the practitioner with knowledge can
Control, summon, and divide,
Kill, expel, and shake,
Immobilize and make stiff,
Confuse, and likewise plant the stake,
Steal the words, make [someone] stupid,
Deaf, and blind,
Make [someone] a hermaphrodite,
Or completely change shape.

These twelve great actions
Are always accomplished by the practitioner,
And the realized practitioner should
Have no doubt that the realizations
Will be attained through mindfulness.

At all the supreme places and so forth
The dakinis are all-pervasive.
Endowed with exalted wisdom of their own birthplace,
They are born in country after country
As the queens of the vajra mandala.

And then the explanation of the dakinis:
[They are in] Kuluta and Maru,

The lands of Sindhu and Nagara,
Suvarnadvipa, Saurashtra,
Grihadevata, Pretapuri,
Himalaya and Kanchi,
The lands of Lampaka and Kalinga,
Koshala and Trishakune,
Otre and Kamarupa,
Malawa and Devikota,
Rameshvara and Godavari,
Arbuta and Oddiyana,
Jalandhara, Pulliramalaya, and so forth.
All the girls of these lands
Are nondual with the hero and yogini.
They have desirous forms and
Will enter through the power of mind.[73]

The six yoginis are in Kuluta,
The mothers in the land of Maru.
Lama [dakinis] are in the land of Sindhu.
The lineage of the principal mother is in Nagara.
In Lampaka and Saurashtra
Are the goddess lineage.

In Pretapuri are Nak Chenmo[74]
Together with the Rupini dakinis.
In the mountain of Himalaya and Kanchi
Is said to be Sabalika.
And in the lands of Panchala, Grihadevata, and Kalinga

73. This verse is often quoted during teachings on the body mandala, which explains that the dakinis, just by seeing the practitioner engaged in Heruka practice, will enter their body with the power and swiftness of mind.
74. The sTog Palace edition reads *nag chen mo*, "great black one"; the Phugdrag edition has the variant *bu mo*. Gray, who also notes the variant *nags chen*, follows the Sanskrit reading "Mahakala," which matches *nag chen* (2007, 334n34).

Are the goddesses who maintain the conducts.
These are explained as the childish girls.[75]

In Koshala are the carnivores.
Likewise in Pretapuri is
The large and powerful Dorje Khandro (Vajradakini).
In Trishakune are Khandaroha.
Likewise in Pulliramalaya and
The Golden Mountain [76] there are
Twenty-one thousand women
Born into the lineage of butchers.

However many other places there are
They are the yoginis of the mandala of
The glorious Heruka.

Shri Heruka, the great churner,
And the principal mothers of that mandala,
These twenty-four dakinis,
Pervade all migrators in the three worlds,
All things animate and inanimate.

This commitment of the dakinis
Is the illusory meditation.
With perfect concentration and
Whatever else is appropriate, it
Should be brought to completion on this earth.

Always concentrating with the mantra and
Wearing the night sky,
If one begins from the left
All the yoginis and the hero will be delighted.

---

75. This line does not appear in the sTog Palace edition.
76. Tib. *gser ri*; David Gray speculatively identifies this as Kanakagiri.

By offering the dance and mudra
And continuously offering the self-arisen,
Everything without exception will be attained
By undertaking offerings from the left.

FROM THE SPEECH OF GLORIOUS HERUKA, "THE RITUAL OF
THE ARRANGEMENT OF THE TWENTY-FOUR MANDALAS" IS
THE FORTY-FIRST CHAPTER.

42. The Ritual of the Laughing Mantra and the Illusory Form of the Yogini

Next, the hero having drunk flower water
Should remember this mantra.
The practitioner dances[77] in this way
Together with his mudra.
By always eating meat at night
And [reciting] the mantra three times
He quickly attains bliss.

Offer drinks in the same way,
Touching and smiling at
The great principal mother.
While practicing brahmin's conduct and
Laughing at the beginning and end with the mudra,
This famous [goddess] looks proudly.
In this way, at night as well as during the day
One should always be laughing.

The hero listens in such a place
To all the secrets of body and actions.
Always crying,
The hair rises out of faith,
Not mounting the vajra
And likewise making offerings naked.

---

77. This word (Skt. *nrityam*) was evidently read as *nityam*, "always" (Tib. *rtag tu*), in the Tibetan text; therefore, here I have followed David Gray's translation of the Sanskrit.

These are the stages of
All the powerful goddesses of desire,
With the collection mudras.
With exhalations, exhortations, and laughter,
The marvelous dance,
And a variety [of other means], induce desire
By remembering mantra and mudra and
Laughing eight times HA HA HE HE.

The supreme joy of the various powerful [goddesses],
Saying HA HA they draw you near.
A tear falls[78] and
Through that you will fall in love,
The perfect union of mantra and concentration.

The hairs of the principal mothers
And the hero rise together in bliss.
Do not mount the vajra
[Of those who] examine the left.

FROM THE SPEECH OF GLORIOUS HERUKA, "THE RITUAL OF
THE LAUGHING MANTRA AND THE ILLUSORY FORM OF THE
YOGINI" IS THE FORTY-SECOND CHAPTER.

78. This reading follows the sTog Palace edition; the Phugdrag edition says, "Always performing, crying, and [reciting] the mantra."

43. The Ritual of Accomplishing the Actions of the Close Essence [Mantra]

Next, the explanation of Chenrezig,[79]
Who is nondual with the hero,
Who knows the ritual for distinguishing the place
And continuously delights in meditation.

At a house, crossroads,
The abode of the hero, or a mountain,
One is seen by the dakinis as abiding in the commitments
Even from a long way off.
Offer a naked [action] mudra.
Through this action you will[80]
Attain the state of sacredness.
Clothes and other coverings
Should not be worn by the desirous ones.
Thus having let down your hair
Commence all actions.

[With] the root mantra as well as others
Bind [those] dwelling in the directions.

79. David Gray says "Chenrezig" (Tib. *spyan ras gzigs*) is a mistranslation of the Sanskrit *alokam* (Tib. *gzigs pa*) on the part of this Tibetan translator, and should instead read "glance," which would change the reading of this verse to "Now I will explain the glance of a man who is nondual with the hero." The way it is translated here is in accordance with the Tibetan text.
80. This reading follows the Phugdrag edition; the sTog Palace edition says, "Led by the hand to the state of sacredness."

The act of offering should not be seen by
The gods or the collection of demigods.

Both hands full of flowers
Should be offered toward the sky.
If those flowers do not fall
And are not seen on the ground,
A thousand dakinis
Abiding in this particular place
Will be subjugated.

The goddess of powerful speech
And the lord of speech will be summoned;
Therefore gradually one will
Come to know conversations of the gods
And know the movement of the stars.

In towns as well as in isolated places,
Those which are underground,[81]
The cities and crossroads,
A tree and the abode of the hero,
Or on the peak of a mountain and in the sky,
By always remembering the essence and close essence [mantras]
Gods and men will not see you.
Through that, the practitioner can always
Stay in these regions.

The nature of the seven-syllable mantra[82]
Visualized as red at the top of a tree,
[That tree] will quickly fall without breaking
But not in other places.

---

81. This line is only in the sTog Palace edition.
82. That is, the close essence mantra of Heruka. This line is from the sTog Palace edition.

Place [the mantra] on your body
And sleep on a cushion of *kusha* grass.
Then one should recite the seven-syllable mantra
One hundred and eight times.

All the activities in your dreams
Will be revealed according to your wishes.
You will destroy untimely death
And all actions will be fulfilled.
A variety of others as well
Will be shown in your dreams.

Also recite the mantra over a sword, water,
Your thumb, a butter lamp, or a mirror.
By the mantra yoga of oneself
You will cause the descent of the *prasena*.[83]
While meditating repeat the recitation seven times
And virtue and nonvirtue will become apparent.

And then divide and arrange
The seven-syllable mantra of the hero.
Imagine it in the center of a sun disk
And recite it up to a thousand [times]
And it will appear [as clear] as a crystal.
[If you] show this to those who are afflicted with illness,
By merely seeing it [the disease] will be cleared.
Have no doubt all illness will be destroyed and
One will be liberated from that illness
Like an autumn moon.

Arrange a wheel on the left hand
In the center of the moon and
The seven syllables that appear like the color of crystal.

83. This Sanskrit term, transliterated in Tibetan, refers to a divinatory object; thanks to David
Gray for this clarification.

Placed upon any diseases,
The contagious diseases, spirits,
And so forth will be obliterated,
As well as all pains and so forth, leprosy,
Poisons, illnesses, and so forth.

Have no doubt that all illnesses
Will be cast to the ten directions
Through imagining the letters on the moon [disk].

In a secret place at night
Crush beef[84] with the three sweets,
Knowing the seven syllables of the secret mantra and
Performing eight thousand burned offerings;
In the morning the mantrika
Will acquire a thousand measures of gold.

By doing ten thousand burned offerings
[He will] acquire a sacred land.
Whatever place he thinks of,
And at any time,
Have no doubt he will take rebirth there
And become a king of secret mantra.

With white [all] becomes peaceful,
With black you can kill in an instant,
With red you can subjugate
And summon in an instant, and
With yellow all will be subdued.
This is the definitive [meaning] of the teachings.

With yellow you can subdue an army,
Overcoming its boats, machines, and elephants.

84. Here, the Tibetan text phoneticizes the Sanskrit *gau-mamsa*, "cowflesh."

By merely thinking of white
The dead are revived.
One who has been captured by one hundred ghosts
Is also quickly revived.

By seeing [someone] who has
Fallen unconscious due to poison,
He will be perfectly awakened and arise.
By seeing one's hand, contagious diseases,
Spirits, and epilepsy[85] become terrified.

While constantly reciting [it] mentally
Throwing dice or fighting with a closed fist,
As long as your clenched fist is not loosened
All activities will be accomplished.

Even if an enemy
Lifts up a weapon in his hand,
As long as your clenched fists are not opened
He will be unable to strike you.

Thus all actions are
Likewise accomplished with
Fruit, flower petals,
Betel nut, and other foods.

The first is the union of the body,
The second is power,
The third is speech,
The fourth is unobservable; [these are all]
Accomplished by the *King of Mantras*.

You will have the power to benefit or curse
The animate and inanimate [beings] of the three realms,

85. Tib. *brjed byed* (Skt. *apasmāra*); according to David Gray, this refers to epilepsy.

In the earth together with the trees,
Or in the ocean or a bound sash,
Have no doubts about these attainments.

FROM THE SPEECH OF GLORIOUS HERUKA, "THE RITUAL
OF ACCOMPLISHING THE ACTIONS OF THE CLOSE ESSENCE
[MANTRA]" IS THE FORTY-THIRD CHAPTER.

44. The Ritual Actions of the Seven Syllables of the Six Dakinis

Then rely on a messenger
Endowed with the seven-syllable mantra
Through which actions are correctly undertaken
And quickly accomplished in an instant.

With the ritual of the seven syllables,
Arrange in the center of your hand[86]
The six dakinis, perfectly abiding in
A wheel endowed with a signal in the left [hand].

Visualizing that which has his form
From the mouth one recites the king of secret mantras;
The one to whom that hand is shown
Will definitely be summoned.

[Mix] the dust of red sandalwood
And likewise black mustard seeds and salt
In the footprint made in the ground by
The object of accomplishment.[87]

Grind it together and
Soften it with both hands.
Perform a burned offering to the yogini

86. The sTog Palace edition does not say "hand."
87. In other words, the one to be summoned.

At night and burn it to dust in the fire of a butcher
Or in a charnel ground fire.

Moving toward the object of accomplishment
And undertaking this yoga,
When you complete one hundred recitations,
He will definitely be summoned.

When one accomplishes this, his self-nature,
His wealth, and living beings will be subjugated.
Accomplish these preparations;
I do not say otherwise.

Take that very powder and
Mix it together with iron powder.
Wrapping it in cloth from the charnel ground
Recite [the mantra] seven times at a crossroad
And dig eight finger-widths into the ground
And hide it together with the name of your enemy.

The person whose name you say
Will quickly be overcome
By reciting over that very powder.

If you enthusiastically [cleanse] it with milk,
He will again come to life;
Have no doubt this will be accomplished.

Take that powder and
Bind it with cloth of the charnel grounds
Possessing the five intoxicants and
Write the name of your enemy.

If you hide that in the charnel grounds
And say the recitation one hundred times,
The victim will become crazy.

By casting it out [he] will be released.
By enthusiastically cleansing it
With the milk of a cow
He will again come to life.
Have no doubt that [this] will be accomplished.

FROM THE SPEECH OF GLORIOUS HERUKA, "THE RITUAL
ACTIONS OF THE SEVEN SYLLABLES OF THE SIX DAKINIS" IS
THE FORTY-FOURTH CHAPTER.

45. The Ritual of the Six Yoginis, the Attainments of Speech, and the Prophecy

Next, the excellent supreme actions that
Accomplish the realizations of speech.

Take one hundred and eight
Red karavira flowers
And vigorously [rinse] them with cow's milk.[88]
Recite [the mantra] one hundred and eight times and
With each recitation hit the head of the penis.[89]
Continue performing in this way
With perfect concentration for seven days.

Then, after eleven days
Take the flowers,
Go to a great river,
Take them all one by one
And throw them in the water,
Perfectly reciting as you take each one.

If the last flower tossed in the water
Reverses its descent and travels upstream,
And if you take that together with some water,
And drink it without biting,

---

88. The word "rinse" is taken from David Gray's translation from the Sanskrit but does not exist in the Tibetan.
89. The text says *lingam*, which is another word for the penis.

The practitioner will accomplish the
Speech arisen from the *Secret Tantra*.

Next, bind the vagina mudra[90]
And recite [the mantra] one hundred and eight times
With the mantrika facing the object of accomplishment.
On the stomach of the object of accomplishment,
Set the mind accordingly, then
The adept moves his little finger
During the three times of the day.
Even if one kills a brahmin
After seven days Indra and so forth are definitely summoned.

With the powder of red sandalwood
On an image of the object of accomplishment
Rub its body with the three spices
And anoint it with beeswax.
The practitioner pierces its
Secret place with a copper needle.
The skilled one should warm it for seven days
With the smokeless charcoal of a *khadira* tree.[91]
At the end of one hundred recitations
The king, minister,
And the queen together with their retinues
Will definitely all be summoned.

Write the name of the king together with his court
On the leaf of a birch tree,
Writing with the tip of a finger of a corpse
And drawing with mental stabilization, then
Recite it a hundred times facing [his] direction.

It is said that to gain accomplishment, recite it
In a charnel ground fire of acacia wood.

90. The Phugdrag edition says "one hundred" (Tib. *brgya*) instead of "mudra" (*rgya*).
91. Tib. *seng ldeng*; an acacia tree. Thanks to David Gray for the name of the tree.

As long as the beeswax [image] does not melt
But becomes warm, the king,
Together with a chakravartin king,
Will also definitely be summoned.

The practitioner should
Take dust from the footprint of
The object of accomplishment,
Add red sandalwood and
Grind it with the leftover
Ashes from the charnel grounds.

Vigorously dried in the flames
Of smokeless acacia charcoal,
Take that dust and soften it
With your two hands and perform the burned offering.

By taking that powder, [they] will remain unmoving;
Hide it, and [they] will be tormented,
Fall unconscious, become senseless,
Confused and deluded, and [they]
Will come with the force of the wind
And throw [themselves] at the practitioner.

[Make them into]
A sacrificial animal or else a female messenger[92]
As discerned by the practitioner.
Then the activities of messengers
Will be captured by these actions.

Take the branch of a moistened karavira tree
The measure of your forearm, and upon it
The practitioner should write the mantra
Together with whatever is to be accomplished.

92. These next two lines are missing from the Phugdrag edition.

Toss it into the flames of a burning corpse
And as long as it is not burned up,
Quickly go and retrieve it.
By reciting the knowledge [mantra] seven times
And circumambulating while reciting,
In that very instant
A beautiful man or woman will be
Drawn to you by the power of the wind.

The practitioner takes a red karavira flower,
Prepared during the lunar conjunction with Gyal (Pushya)
with one hundred recitations,
And smears it with [blessed] cow product
And places it in flower water.

One enters the force of a great river
Up to the navel and,
Standing in the center with your hands cupped,
Recites the knowledge [mantra] a thousand times.
Filling both hands,
Drink this [flower] together with the water.
Through this the practitioner
Will obtain the attainment of speech.

Thus will a king and queen
Definitely be summoned by the mind and
Gods together with demigods and men
Will quickly be subjugated.

[You can] kill with wrathful words;
So too can dividing and expelling
Both be accomplished with words.

By mere words, rivers and
Chariots, machines, and oceans,
Oxen, horses, and likewise clouds,

People, or even birds can be suppressed.
All beings and all wishes
Will all be accomplished by the mind.

Next, the application of summoning
And copulating with all women.
Properly take the red karavira flower and
Recite the knowledge [mantra] a hundred times
And place it in the center of her vagina
And enclose that flower.
Definitely arrange it in [her] secret place.

Endowed with the yoga of the nondual exalted wisdom,
Recite the mantra a hundred times over
The flower in the center of [her] vagina.

The practitioner should extract one [flower].
Whoever is struck by that flower
Will instantly come under your control and
Fall unconscious and senseless.

All of her limbs and joints
Are controlled by another, as well as
The collection of limbs and other powers;
Her confidence[93] is reversed
And instantly she comes under your power.
This is the attainment of confidence
And the meaning of subjugation.

FROM THE SPEECH OF GLORIOUS HERUKA, "THE RITUAL OF
THE SIX YOGINIS, THE ATTAINMENTS OF SPEECH, AND THE
PROPHECY" IS THE FORTY-FIFTH CHAPTER.

93. This term was taken from David Gray's translation.

46. The Ritual of the Actions of the Five HA Syllables

Next, by merely knowing the five syllables
That accomplish all actions
You will quickly attain the realizations.

HAM HOU HO HAI HAH

The five signal HA syllables are
Softened by the hand.
When blood comes from his mouth
In that instant the enemy dies.

Taking one's own blood and
Rubbing a skull with the ring finger,
As soon as it dries
You will destroy the object of accomplishment.

If one is blazing with anger
And recites with reddened eyes,
The king will quickly die together with
His army and his mount.

A cat, a jewel-spitting mongoose,
A raven, fox, and water fowl:
Preparing the powerful dakinis,
These are quickly attained.
Have no doubts about this tantra.

Make a thread of rabbit hairs
And recite [the mantra] a thousand times.
Whoever's neck it is tied to
Becomes like that.

Reciting [it] a thousand times in the hand and
While reciting each letter,
Take the karavira flower.

If you touch a pregnant mother
The child is expelled from the womb
And when released there is liberation.

To whomever one makes
A threatening mudra, that one will die,
And again that one will be brought back to life.

FROM THE SPEECH OF GLORIOUS HERUKA, "THE RITUAL OF
THE ACTIONS OF THE FIVE HA LETTERS" IS THE FORTY-SIXTH
CHAPTER.

47. The Ritual of All the Actions of the Mantra of the Dakini of All the Buddhas

Next, a further perfect explanation,
The essence of all the dakinis.
By merely reciting this
All the realizations will be born.

Next, if one recites the great knowledge [mantra] of the dakinis, one will accomplish the subjugation of all lineages. If one constantly recites [the mantra], great glory is generated. With a ritual dagger made of human bone six finger [widths] in length, recite it one hundred and eight times. [Whoever's] doorway you hide it in, his lineage will be annihilated. [Bury it] in a field for water buffalo, elephants, or horses, dig in that place, and if it is hidden there, they will all be destroyed.

And then if one desires that the king or the king's minister be controlled, the adept should make a mirror image of him from clay, eight fingers long, and hide it in the doorway of the kingdom. On the first day mix *lunga* flowers[94] together with fruits and saffron and perform one thousand burned offerings and he will be subjugated. By this mantra one can summon, subdue, confuse, emaciate, bewitch, steal words, blind, and intoxicate, as well as dispel.

And then, the actions to perform if one wishes to be born as a woman: Assemble flowers and the fruit from a *kakandaki* tree and equal portions of a crow, [namely] the claw, the skin from the lower part of the feet, and the blood, as well as the blood of a rabbit. Grind them up into eleven pills, which are then dried in the shade. Similarly, on a good day bind them to

94. Tib. *lung ka,* referring to *matulunga,* or the citron tree.

your hands, and whomever's head it is placed upon, on the twelfth day they will become a woman.

Then, if one wishes to be born a dog, you should take Gyal (Pushya) skymetal[95] and place it on the head of a jewel-spitting mongoose and perform eight thousand burned offerings over seven nights.[96]

On the eighth day, with equal portions of saffron, recite [the mantra] one hundred and eight times and perform a burned offering with that powder. The one upon whose head you place that dust will become a dog. To restore him again, at night time make a great offering to the dakinis and offer tormas and he will transform back to his natural state.

For one who desires to become material or immaterial, offer a hundred and eight burned offerings of the fruit of a golden tree and one will become immaterial. If one performs a burned offering of *arura* fruit, he will return to his natural state.

It is said that if one wishes to make [someone] crazy, perform the burned offering in the place of a great bird.[97] If you do this, then on the seventh day [he] will become crazy. If you wish to restore him, offer rice husks in the burned offering and he will be pacified.

Perform a burned offering with the hair of a cat during a lunar eclipse while saying that person's name together with the mantra. Take the ash [from the burned offering] and place it on their head and they will become a cat. Recite it again and he will return to his natural state.

With a string made of crow intestines, perform the recitation. Whomever's neck you tie it around will become a crow. Anyone whose neck is bound with whatever intestines that have been [blessed] with [mantra] recitation will become just like that [aspect]. Likewise, they will take on the form of a dove, peacock, water fowl, owl, hawk, vulture, or dog. With a string of ox hair, say the recitation one hundred and eight times, and then if it is tied around someone's neck they will transform into an ox. If a thread of hair made from any four-legged animal and so forth is bound

95. The sTog Palace edition reads *skar ma rgyal gyi gnam lcags*. The underlying term (Skt. *puṣya-loha*) may refer to meteoric iron, perhaps specifically a piece that fell during the conjunction of this particular lunar mansion, as Gray speculates (2007, 362n15).

96. The sTog Palace edition says "recite eight thousand recitations."

97. Tib. *bya chen po*; Skt. *mahāśakuna*. Gray (2007, 363) cites Indian commentaries that suggest this may refer to an owl or crow.

to the neck of another, they will transform into that [animal]; if untied, they will become liberated. Recite it on unhusked grain and put it on the house of a great being, and then bestow empowerments upon oneself with the remnants for seven nights and all of his grain will be summoned.

FROM THE SPEECH OF GLORIOUS HERUKA, "THE RITUAL OF ALL THE ACTIONS OF THE MANTRA OF THE DAKINI OF ALL THE BUDDHAS" IS THE FORTY-SEVENTH CHAPTER.

48. The Ritual of the Secret Abode of All the Heroes and Yoginis

Next, the further explanation of
The virtuous dance of all the dakinis.[98]
The essence of all the yoginis
Accomplishes all the desired aims,
Which by merely remembering
Shakes the three worlds,
And by mere subsequent mindfulness
One will perfectly accomplish the stages.

HA SÖ PHAT HUM HUM YE NI NA WA VAJRA YE NI KI DA
BUDDHA SARWA OM

By reciting this mantra you will receive attainments,
It is the accomplishment of all virtuous actions
Of the dakinis.
This mantra is famed as
The essence of the yoginis [such as]
Khandaroha, Lama, and so forth.

The dakinis and yoginis,
Below the ground as well as in the heavens,
Likewise those in the lands of men
And whatever actions there are,
Through this mantra they are all accomplished.

98. The Phugdrag edition says "that which is virtuous for all dakinis."

This is the virtuous means of attainments
Bestowing all attainments.

Other than this, there is nothing more sublime
Existing in the three worlds.
For which purpose this is unexcelled.
All the actions will be accomplished
And the excellent method of the deity is revealed.

[Now] I will explain the abode of
All the dakinis, briefly but not extensively.

One should draw an excellent mountain
With a variety of fruits and flowers.
Continuously meditate that upon these are
The dakinis such as Lama,
Khandaroha, and Dakini.

The hero of the heroes
Saying HA HA HE HE,
Heruka is the net of the dakinis,
Of the twenty-four heroes:
Dorje Sempa (Vajrasattva), Nam Nang (Vairochana),
Pema Karwang (Padmanarteshvara), Pel Traktung (Shri Heruka),
Khanying (Akashagarbha), and Tamdrin (Hayagriva),
Rinchen Dorje (Ratnavajra), Tobpoché (Mahabala),
Mik Misang (Virupaksha), Jikché (Bhairava),
Dorje Sangpo (Vajrabhadra), Rabsang (Subhadra),
Dorje Humdze (Vajrahumkara), Pawoche (Mahavira),
Dorje Relpachen (Vajrajatila), Myuguchen (Ankurika),
Dorje Lü (Vajradehaka), Dorje Öd (Vajraprabha),
Ödpakme (Amitabha) and the Lhayi Dra (Suravairi),
Likewise, Chewa Nampartsik (Vikatadamstrina),
Kengru (Kankala), Kengru Chenpo (Mahakankala),
Thöpay Dumbu (Khandakapala), and so forth.

The twenty-four heroes,
The heroes and dakinis
Pervade all these migrators.
The yoginis, Rabtuma (Prachanda) and so forth
Should be seen as abiding in the mandala.
In all actions performed, the practitioner,
Desiring power, should continuously meditate
With excellent meditative concentration
On the nature of the mandala.

The ritual previously explained,
Proclaimed by Heruka, the net of the dakinis,
Abiding in all the attainments of the great mandala,
Is the basis of all attainments.

It was perfectly explained by the ten million
Buddhas and ten million heroes.
Each of the dakinis
Is always attended by ten million
Yoginis and dakinis:
The yoginis and dakinis
Suk Chenma (Rupini) and Dum Kyema (Khandaroha),
Likewise Lama, and so forth.
These accomplish the virtuous actions of the practitioner.

FROM THE SPEECH OF GLORIOUS HERUKA, "THE RITUAL OF
THE SECRET ABODE OF ALL THE HEROES AND YOGINIS" IS
THE FORTY-EIGHTH CHAPTER.

49. The Ritual of Accomplishing the Complete Exchange of Form of the Seven-Birthed One

Next, further explanation according to
The ritual for accomplishing the sacrificial animal,
By merely knowing which
The realizations are quickly attained.

The mantrika should make the form of a sacrificial animal
With rice powder according to the stages:
A person, a turtle, and a camel,
A donkey, a wolf, a horse, and so forth,
And likewise a mottled pig.
One should know these sacrificial animals.
From these I will explain the actions
In accordance with their characteristics.

One birth and two births,
Three, four, or five,
Six rebirths or seven,
Have no doubt these are the sacrificial animals.[99]

Whoever has a sweet taste in their mouth,
Looks without blinking,
Speaks the truth, and looks [upon others] with love,
Always delighting in the holy Dharma;

99. Despite the fact that at this point a person is being described, I have left it as "sacrificial animal" (Tib. *phyugs bsgrub bya*) in accordance with the Tibetan text.

He knows his own birth,
His body always smells sweet:
The one endowed with these characteristics
Is the one arisen for seven births.

By merely eating
Smelling or touching that
You will transform into the form of a god.

Make that into a drop and
You will instantly receive attainments
And will quickly arise in that form.

The adept takes the heart
And recites the mantra.
By reciting the essence mantra
On that, make it into a drop, and
Whatever the form of that living being
Have no doubt you will be transformed
Into that aspect through this drop.

The adept takes the sap of a tree
And places the drop on the forehead;
Whatever form you wish for
Have no doubt you will transform into that form.

Bind your hands and the crown of your head
With the hair of the sacrificial animal.
If you mix his hairs
Together with his five limbs[100] and
Bind it to the hands [and] the top of the head,
Have no doubt you will change into that form.

---

100. Tib. *yan lag lnga*; Skt. *pañcāṅga*. On interpretations of this term by Indian commentators, see Gray 2007, 368n8.

Through meditation and recitation on yoga,
Possessing human potential yet
Delighting in the austerities and delusions,
This will block the path to realizations.

Elephants, horses, and donkeys,
Turtles, camels, pigs, and foxes,
Crows, owls, and so forth, vultures,
Cranes,[101] falcons, and a curlew,
Assuming good forms and bad forms
Or the form of a god,
Have no doubt that the yogi is the
Great hero who will assume this form.

Through this you will accomplish the utmost supreme
That does not exist in the three worlds.

FROM THE SPEECH OF GLORIOUS HERUKA, "THE RITUAL OF ACCOMPLISHING THE COMPLETE EXCHANGE OF FORM OF THE SEVEN-BIRTHED ONE" IS THE FORTY-NINTH CHAPTER.

---

101. Tib. *sa ra sa* [var. *la*]; here I follow Gray (2007, 369n12), who reads this as a transliteration of Skt. *sārasa*.

50. The Ritual of the Controlling Burned Offering and Teaching on the Abodes of the Grounds and So Forth

Next, through the ritual of the burned offering
You will definitely accomplish control.
And it is taught that if the ritual is done correctly
Realization will quickly be accomplished.

If you mix beef with intoxicants
And perform the burned offering with the left hand,
The buddhas will definitely be subjugated; [therefore,]
What need is there to mention an insignificant person?

The three realms will be subjugated
With saliva, tree splinters, and
Likewise what is pleasing to one's own body as well as
Intoxicants together with the name of the [victim].

In an instant they will be summoned with
Blood from the sign of the moon[102] and
Food moistened by eating
Together with human hair.

In an instant they will be separated by
The adept performing a burned offering with
Vomit from his own body

102. Menstrual blood.

And his own hair and through
Performing the burned offering
With the burning wood from a *nimba* tree.

[He] will immediately be killed or expelled
With meditative stabilizations.
In a fire [made from] *datura*,
Mustard seed oil, and a wing of an aged crow,
Perform the burned offering.

If the adept always recites the mantra,
Obstructions will not exist for that one
While sleeping, not sleeping,
Eating, [engaged] in union, and so forth.

After three months
The poverty of his lineage will be destroyed
By one hundred sacrificial offerings of fox meat,
And by the one who performs the sacrificial offerings properly.

In all places where one performs the burned offering
With the great meats and intoxicants
Up to one hundred and eight [times],
All those places where the practitioner has performed
[That burned offering] during the three periods
For six months, will be subdued.
That will satiate the dakinis, who will
Undoubtedly give him a kingdom.

By meditating on all deities while
Performing the burned offering during the two parts of the day,
You will obtain [the ability] to travel in the sky
With your own body.
With jackal meat and wine
Perform the outer and inner burned offering.

This will quickly bring to hand
An engagement with the best attainments.

By reciting the mantra at night
The surrounding area will be summoned.
If you do this everyday
You will also become a king.
There is nothing more supreme than this in the three worlds.
The great yogi's own death will be as he pleases
And will manifest in a variety of forms.

If one performs one hundred thousand
Burned offerings with wood-apple (*bilva*), a *palasha* tree,
And *udubvara*, one will
Quickly become a lord of great wealth.[103]

With mixed beef and intoxicants,
The burned offering should be done by one who desires a kingdom.
If pleasing the powerful yogi
How could one become poor?

By burning jackal [flesh]
What [you desire] is easily obtained.
By offering jackal [flesh]
You will quickly become a lord of wealth.
Even if you don't observe the conducts purely,
You quickly obtain the realizations of [this] teaching.

To extend one's life take
Wax gourd,[104] chickpea,
Honey, husks, mustard grain,

103. For a description of these three plants, see Gray 2007, 372–73.
104. The Tibetan text transliterates Skt. *kuṣmāṇḍa*. Thanks to David Gray for the name of this substance.

And the limbs of a *tamala* tree,
And bind one's mouth.
The yogi will enjoy one's desires
And abide on the Joyous [ground].[105]

OM VAJRA BEROTZANIYE HUM HUM PHAT SÖHA[106]

And then, further explanation of
The grounds and abodes of the yoginis:
The limbs of Heruka's body are
The nature of all things stable and moving.

The seat is the Very Joyous ground,
Likewise the adjacent seat is the Stainless,
This field is the Illuminating,
The close-place is the Radiant,
The *tsandoha*[107] is the Manifest,
The close *tsandoha* is the Difficult to Overcome,
The gathering place is the Gone Afar,
The close gathering is the Unshakeable,
The charnel ground is the Good Intelligence, and
The close charnel ground is the Cloud of Dharma.[108]

Through the teaching and practice of Shri Heruka
The grounds abide within oneself.
The grounds of the ten perfections are in
The symbolic language of the yoginis.

In the heavens above, on the earth, and below,
The limbs of the hero are the nature

---

105. Tib. *rab tu dga' ba*; Skt. *pramuditā*. This is the first of the ten bodhisattva grounds.
106. This mantra appears in the Phugdrag edition but not in the sTog Palace edition.
107. On the possible origins and meaning of this transliterated term, see Gray 2007, 374n39.
108. This stanza establishes the relationship between the ten bodhisattva grounds and the ten types of pilgrimage place. The fifth and sixth bodhisattva grounds have been reversed from their usual order. For a schematic description of these correspondences, see Gray 2007, 67.

Of all things stable and moving;
Revealed as Pulliramalaya and so forth,
They are [both] the inner and outer abode of oneself.

The great king, the *Glorious Drinker of Blood,*
The principal lord of all desires,
[He] is everywhere, in the hands and feet,
In every eye, face, and hand,
Every hearer in the world.
His abode covers all things.

You will accomplish all the attainments
With the mind endowed with concentration.
For the sake of benefiting the practitioner
I have taught this secret.

FROM THE SPEECH OF GLORIOUS HERUKA, "THE RITUAL
OF THE CONTROLLING BURNED OFFERING AND TEACHING
ON THE ABODES OF THE GROUNDS AND SO FORTH" IS THE
FIFTIETH CHAPTER.

51. [Untitled Final Chapter]

And then the supreme explanation of that[109]
The oral instructions are very difficult to find,
The symbolic language of the hero
I have hidden in the *Tantra*.
The garments, five mudras, and so forth,
Branches of wisdom, the tent and dagger.
Through reciting the *Ali-Kali*[110]
The cause and so forth, are preceded by emptiness.

By the *nada* entering and so forth,[111]
Until the yoga of absorption,
Nectar that satisfies and brings liberation,
Bestowing initiation, and the hand offering.

Also, by the great armor of perfect protection,
And making offerings with all the mantras,
In that way, these are the fourteen essential topics
I have briefly explained.[112]

---

109. In the Phugdrag edition it says, "Furthermore it is taught," but here, given that the fifty-first chapter is a summary, I am assuming when the sTog Palace edition says "of that" (Tib. *de yi*), it is referring to the previous fifty chapters.

110. I left the terms *Ali-Kali* (as they are transliterated in the Tibetan text) for poetic meter. These terms are the standard Tibetan way of referring to vowels and consonants, respectively.

111. Here, the term in question is literally "sound" (Tib. *sgra*), but as explained in Tibetan commentaries it is a reference to the *nada*—that is, the nasal sound represented by a semicircle.

112. For an explanation of these fourteen essential topics, see Sermey Khensur Lobsang Tharchin, *Sublime Path to Kechara Paradise* (Howell, NJ: Mahayana Sutra and Tantra Press, 1997), 10.

Those supreme people who perform every action,
Completely purifying all negativities of the self,
Will attain the ground of a tathagata, and
Life after life will be born into the lineage of the Buddha
And become a king endowed with faith.

The characteristics of all the previously
Accumulated negative karma will lessen.
For those who continuously meditate
All of your wishes will be accomplished.

For example, if a container filled with butter
Is placed in the middle of a fire,
The fresh butter on top will melt and
Destroy the impurities of that container.

In the same way Shri Heruka
Will destroy the signs of nonvirtue.

By merely remembering, concentrating,
Reading, reciting, or writing,
You will attain the enjoyments of the pure lands
Or the state of a chakravartin king.

The yogi will be transferred [to the pure land] with
The *Drinker of Blood* as well as the yogini,
With a variety of flowers held in their hands,
Possessing a variety of victory banners and pendants,

With the sound of a variety of music,
And offering various sounds, [they]
Will lead you to the pure land of the dakinis.
In this way death will be a [mere] conceptualization.

On this earth it is difficult to find
This great tantra of the most glorious Heruka.

For those who know of this yet lack faith,
Those poor beings will be tormented.
For them suffering will always arise.

A necklace, bracelets, armlets,
Earrings, and a brahmin's thread,
A noose, trident, and a rosary of human heads,
A girdle and small bells creating sounds.

On a lotus of various colors atop Mount [Meru]
In the center of which the *Ali-Kali* are generated,
Assuming the aspect of subduing Gauri's Lord,[113]
Embracing [Vajravarahi] and holding a vajra and bell.

Meditate on the supreme state of
The great king, glorious Heruka
Endowed with twelve limbs[114]
And the twenty-four heroes and yoginis.

All the heroes and yoginis,
The retinue unified in the center,
Joyfully become nondual,
Sending out and collecting,

[Fulfilling] the many wishes of sentient beings,
Teaching with various activities,
Subduing in a variety of ways,
And displaying a variety of methods.

Even though one may have no devotion for
The explanation of this profound Dharma,
They should not criticize it
[But should] contemplate this inconceivable Dharma.

113. Tib. *dkar mo bdag po*; Skt. *gauryāḥ patim*. According to Gray (2007, 380n15), this refers to the deities under Heruka's feet—that is, Bhairava and Kalaratri.
114. The text says "half of twenty-four," referring to the number of arms of Heruka.

For the person [for whom] self is not an object,
For him reality is not known, but
It is known by the complete Buddha and his spiritual sons.

Have the buddhas arisen
Or did they all never arise?
The sphere of reality is inconceivable;
Abandon dwelling in either increasing or diminishing.

Even though we establish [reality] in that way,
Do not completely diminish worldly [views].
The transcendent method is beyond thought;
The play of the buddhas inconceivable.

The divisions of the sutra class,
action, performance, and
Yoga and highest yoga tantra:
Those sentient beings that enter [this path] with devotion
Bring happiness according to their wishes.

Colophon

This is the definitive expression of glorious Heruka, the great king of tantra, that was extracted from the *One Hundred Thousand* [*Verse Tantra*] that establishes that which is the most amazing and wonderful; and it is the king of all discourses read by the great hero, glorious Heruka. It is not accomplished by the omniscience of other practitioners and is the unsurpassed attainment from the beginning.

THIS CONCLUDES THE FIFTY-FIRST CHAPTER OF THE DEFINITIVE EXPRESSION OF GLORIOUS HERUKA, THE GREAT KING OF YOGINI TANTRAS.

The Dechen Ling Practice Series

Manjushri's Innermost Secret
A Profound Commentary of Oral Instructions on the Practice of Lama Chöpa
Kachen Yeshe Gyaltsen
Foreword by Ganden Tripa Lobsang Tenzin
Now available from Wisdom Publications

The Essence of the Vast and Profound
A Commentary on Je Tsongkhapa's Middle-Length Treatise on the Stages of the Path to Enlightenment
Pabongkha Rinpoche
Now available from Wisdom Publications

The Extremely Secret Dakini of Naropa
Vajrayogini Practice and Commentary
Pabongkha Rinpoche
Now available from Wisdom Publications

The Chakrasamvara Root Tantra
The Speech of Glorious Heruka
Now available from Wisdom Publications

The Roar of Thunder
Yamantaka Practice and Commentary
Ngulchu Dharmabhadra
and the Fifth Ling Rinpoche, Losang Lungtog Tenzin Trinley

Source of Supreme Bliss
Heruka Chakrasamvara Five-Deity Practice
Ngulchu Dharmabhadra,
and the First Panchen Lama, Losang Chökyi Gyaltsen

Secret Revelations of Chittamani Tara
Generation and Completion Stage Practice and Commentary
Pabongkha Rinpoche

The Blazing Inner Fire of Bliss and Emptiness
An Experiential Commentary on the Practice of the Six Yogas of Naropa
Ngulchu Dharmabhadra

The Melodious Drum of Dakini Land
A Commentary to the Extensive Dedication Prayer of Venerable Vajrayogini
Yangchen Drupai Dorje

Healing Nectar of Immortality
White Tara Healing and Longevity Practices and Commentary
Trijang Rinpoche and Aku Sherab Gyatso

The Ecstatic Dance of Chakrasamvara
Heruka Body Mandala Practice and Commentary
Trijang Rinpoche
Foreword by Gen Lobsang Choephel

About Wisdom Publications

Wisdom Publications is the leading publisher of classic and contemporary Buddhist books and practical works on mindfulness. To learn more about us or to explore our other books, please visit our website at wisdomexperience.org or contact us at the address below.

Wisdom Publications
199 Elm Street
Somerville, MA 02144 USA

We are a 501(c)(3) organization, and donations in support of our mission are tax deductible.

Wisdom Publications is affiliated with the Foundation for the Preservation of the Mahayana Tradition (FPMT).